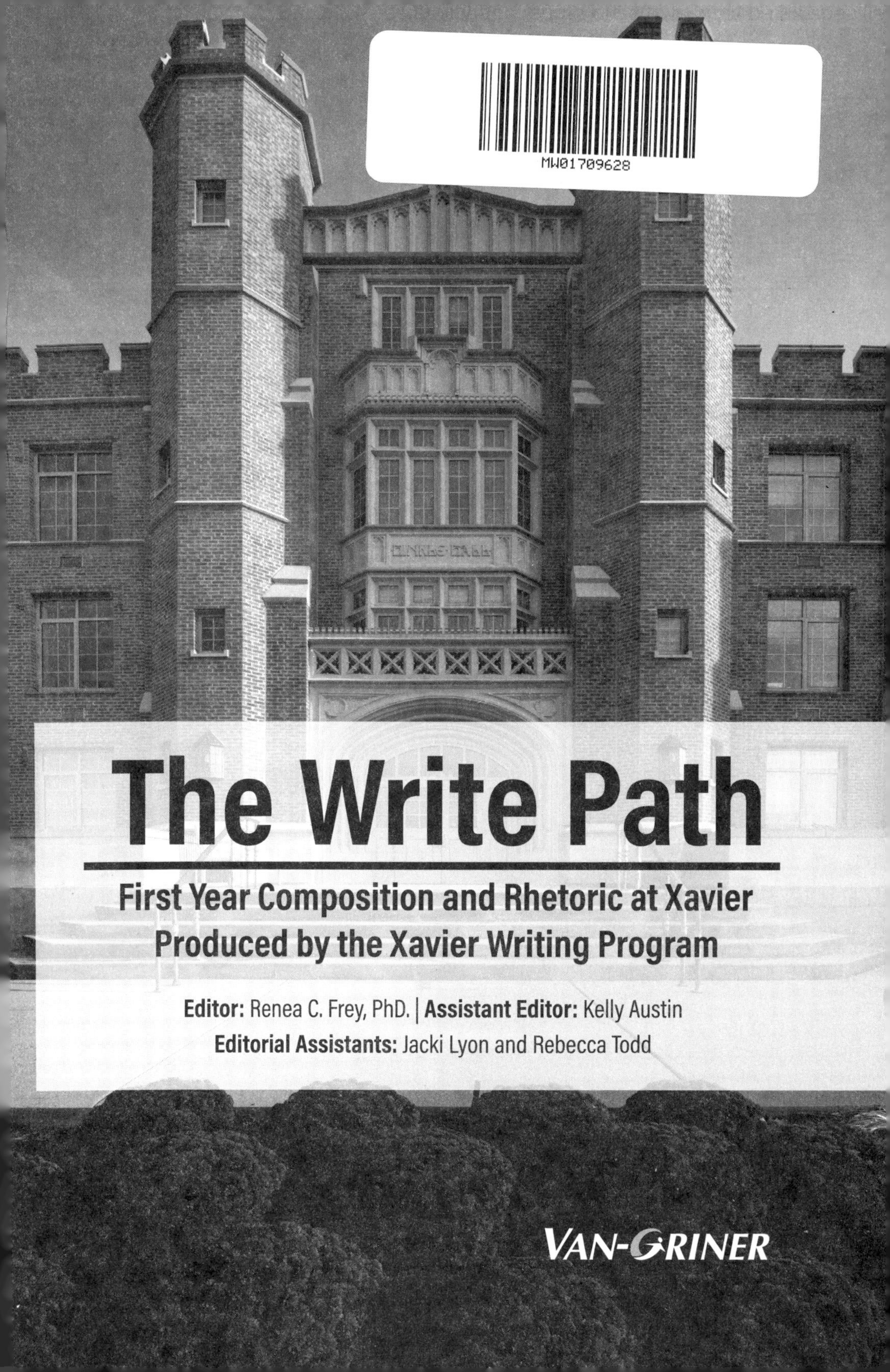

The Write Path

First Year Composition and Rhetoric at Xavier
Produced by the Xavier Writing Program

Editor: Renea C. Frey, PhD. | **Assistant Editor:** Kelly Austin
Editorial Assistants: Jacki Lyon and Rebecca Todd

VAN-GRINER

The Write Path

First Year Composition and Rhetoric at Xavier
Produced by the Xavier Writing Program

Printed in the United States of America
10 9 8 7 6 5 4 3 2 1
ISBN: 978-1-61740-367-5

Van-Griner Publishing
Cincinnati, Ohio
www.van-griner.com

CEO: Mike Griner
President: Dreis Van Landuyt
Project Manager: Maria Walterbusch
Customer Care Lead: Julie Reichert

Frey 367-5 Su16
167350

VAN-GRINER

Table of Contents

Acknowledgments

I would like to thank Xavier's English Department, the Writing Center, and the College of Arts and Sciences Dean's office for supporting this project, as well as Rebecca Todd for coming up with the name for the award and her invaluable help and advice. I would also like to thank Kelly Austin, Jacki Lyon, and Rebecca Todd for their time judging entries and helping to compile this book, with an additional acknowledgement to Kelly for her help proofreading, advising, and selecting award winners. Perhaps most importantly, thanks to all of the student writers from ENGL 101 and 115 who submitted work to make this publication possible.

Welcome!

As first year writers at Xavier, you may have questions or concerns about writing in your college courses. You may love to write and be excited about the new forms of composing you will learn in college or in your major, or you may feel intimidated and uncertain about what to expect. This book is designed to give you more information about writing in college and offer some examples of what successful college-level writing looks like, straight from Xavier students themselves.

In the first section of this book, you will find information about terms, ideas, and practices that will help you succeed with college-level writing and orient you to policies and resources for writing here at Xavier. As you read, you may find that you have heard some of this information before, though other parts may be entirely new. Words such as *rough draft*, *peer response*, and *rhetorical appeals* are likely to play a big part in your writing process in college, so being familiar with the meanings of these words can help you find your way in your writing courses. Additionally, this text will cover issues of academic honesty, plagiarism, and how to properly cite sources in research-based writing so that you can create quality work that acknowledges information you have learned from outside sources. Resources such as the Writing Center and Library will also be explained so that you know where to turn when you need additional support and information for your writing.

In the second section, you can read selected essays from first year students at Xavier who, like you, were recently in ENGL 101 or ENGL 115 working on similar assignments. Looking through their work, you can see what type of writing is expected so that you can better understand the genres you will be asked to write in your first year writing courses. You may have seen some of these before—such as a research-based argument—but you will be prompted to examine the writing more deeply with questions at the end of each essay, so that you can more fully appreciate the "how" and "what" of research writing. Other genres—such as the rhetorical analysis or narrative argument—may be less familiar, and seeing examples can give you an idea of what to expect from these assignments. These examples are not meant to be copied, nor do they represent a rigid set of expectations for an assignment, but rather offer a model of one way that this type of writing can be successfully crafted.

As you write papers in your ENGL 101 or 115 courses, be on the lookout for papers you wrote particularly well and consider submitting them for consideration for the D'Artagnan Award and next year's *Write Path* publication. By submitting your work, you can support and encourage students who, like you, will be first year college writers next year. What you learn now can benefit your fellow students in the future, so please pass along your wisdom and work.

Everyone arrives at college with different backgrounds, experiences, and types of education. This book has been created to help put you on the "write path" in your first year as a Xavier student and to answer questions you may have about writing in college. Also, if there is anything that would have benefitted you that was not included in this book, please let me know so that we can consider including it next year.

Good luck in your first year writing classes!

Sincerely,
Dr. Renea Frey
Writing Program Director

Introduction to The Write Path

College Writing—What Makes it Different?

Nearly everyone does some sort of writing in high school, but what kind and amount of work you do may vary greatly from place to place. In your first year of college, one of the educational goals is to give all students a solid, common foundation in particular subjects, including writing, which can help you for the rest of the time you are at Xavier.

A common genre that students often learn in high school is the five-paragraph essay. While many of the conventions for this type of writing may transfer to college writing, you will also be expected to move beyond the five-paragraph essay to write more complex, longer assignments. In many cases, you will be building upon writing skills you have already learned in high school and expanding them to fulfill new, more in-depth writing prompts.

For instance, you will still need to make strong, focused thesis statements in your work where you give the reader an overview of the claims you will be making in your work, and then organize the rest of your paper around supporting that claim with evidence. In most cases, you will also include elements like topic sentences that announce the content of a paragraph and transitions that allow the reader to easily follow your thought process. You should have a strong conclusion that gives the reader a "call to action" or explains the larger implications of your work, or clarifies why thinking about this issue or text in this way matters. While many of these conventions may be similar to what you have done in high school, it is likely that your instructors in college will ask for greater detail, more depth, additional outside sources, and longer length papers than you typically worked on in high school.

Some other differences in college writing include:

- The type of evidence that "counts" in some assignments may include peer-reviewed scholarly sources, which are written by and for academics in specific disciplines. These pieces may be longer than popular articles, include more field-specific jargon, and be challenging to interpret for those who are new to a discipline.
- You will likely need to offer multiple perspectives in your work, including counter-arguments to your position or refutations of competing perspectives. It is not enough to only argue *your* side—you need to view, and fairly represent, issues from multiple positions.
- In some cases, you may be asked to write from a formal third-person perspective, but in other cases, such as narratives or auto-ethnographies, you may have to write in first-person, beginning your thoughts with "I."
- You will likely write for different audiences, some of which may be a community of scholars, whereas other times, you may be writing for the public.

- Different disciplines have different conventions, citation systems (e.g., MLA, Chicago, or APA), and expectations. As you write for different courses from across the university, you will find that writing varies between disciplines and that what counts as "good writing" may vary in each class.
- How you conduct research, integrate quotes, and cite sources in your work may be more rigorous than what was expected in high school. As you enter college-level work, you become a part of a community of scholars who have high standards for academic integrity and attribution for work and ideas. (More on this topic later ….)

Even if you found writing in high school easy, the writing (and thinking) you will do in college will expand your previous skills. In addition, you will be writing for new audiences, about novel topics, and asked to engage in assignments that will likely push beyond the work you did in high school. This learning can be both challenging and exciting, and the work you do in your first year writing courses serves as a foundation for the writing you will do during your entire time at Xavier.

Process Writing

How many of us have waited to start a writing assignment until the night before, and then frantically wrote all night, quickly proofread the paper once or twice, and then turned it in at the last minute? While this may succeed in "getting the work done," few people (despite the claims every instructor hears) actually produce their best work under these circumstances.

A common practice in ENGL 101 and 115 courses will be to engage in process-based writing. In this approach, instead of having writing assignments where you write on your own, turn in your writing, and then receive a grade, you will work on your writing gradually, in stages, with feedback from peers and/or your instructor at multiple points along the way. In many of your other courses, you will still be asked to create writing where the final *product* is what counts, but in your first year writing courses, we will also focus on the *process*.

Some of you may already be familiar with peer review—sharing your work with classmates to receive feedback and suggestions for revision—but in first year writing, this may be more directed and involve particular practices, such as reading out loud, filling out a worksheet based upon the writing you read, or writing a reflection about what you changed in response to your peer's suggestions. In addition, you may receive feedback from your instructor at various points in your composing process, or be asked to submit a proposal, outline, or research plan for your projects. By focusing on the process, your instructor can guide you as you draft, review, revise, redraft, and revise your papers again.

A process-based approach to writing may include all or some of the following steps:

- Invention work, including brainstorming, heuristics, listing, free-writing, or other exercises to start you thinking about a topic
- Proposals or research plans that ask for details about what, how, and when you intend to create a project

- Annotated bibliographies, which require you to document, summarize, and analyze the sources you are exploring for your research
- Exploratory Essays (sometimes called Synthesis Essays) may be assigned, which will ask you to discuss all of the sources you have examined for your research and reflect upon how what you have learned informs your thinking about your topic
- Outlines or zero drafts where you begin the initial stages of your paper but have not yet composed a full copy
- Rough or first drafts that include all of your completed ideas but that are not yet in the "polished" stage of drafting
- Final or polished drafts that represent your best work, which has been revised, edited, and proofread after receiving input from peers, your instructor, and/or the Writing Center
- Reflections on your writing process, revisions, or finished work

Throughout this process, your instructor may choose various places to intervene, read your current work, and offer feedback or direction. Your peers, too, may be a part of this process, in both formal peer reviews and informal discussions in class. Unlike many of your other courses, your instructor may give you points along the way for different stages of drafting—your finished paper may not be the only writing that "counts" toward your grade.

For many reasons, it is important to keep up with this process as it is outlined in your class schedule. First, it may affect the grade you receive on the overall assignment, especially if various drafts have point values assigned to them. Second, in a course that utilizes peer review, it is important that everyone have a draft to share so that participation is fair and possible. Third, by receiving feedback along the way, you can be more confident that you are fulfilling the assignment correctly and change course sooner if you find that you are not. Lastly, composing your work in steps, even if it is unfamiliar to you, will give you new, valuable skills that you can use in other courses.

Though many students can get into the habit of writing their entire paper quickly the night before, to succeed in college-level writing, it is imperative to take more time planning, drafting, and revising your work. Even the very best writers who are accustomed to receiving A's for their work can benefit from feedback and revision. Additionally, as you progress in your college education, you will encounter assignments that simply cannot be completed in one or two sittings. In order to produce your best work, as well as reduce needless stress, it is important to get into the habit of working on writing assignments in stages, over time.

When we "re-vise" we are actually "re-visioning" or re-seeing our work with fresh eyes. If writing assignments are put off until the last minute, there simply is no time to do this, nor is there space to receive feedback, visit the Writing Center, or read work out loud in order to catch errors in wording.

For these reasons, your first year writing courses will engage writing as process in some manner. This may be a new approach, or it may simply expand your past experiences. Either way, learning to see writing as an ongoing process will save you time, stress, and disappointment in the long run, and support your work in other courses. ENGL 101 and 115 encourage a foundation for best practices in writing that will serve you throughout your college career and beyond.

Rhetoric and Rhetorical Theory

You have likely heard the word "rhetoric" many times in your life, often in a derogatory manner that implies "merely words" or words without honesty or substance. Rhetoric, which will be addressed in both ENGL 101 and 115, is actually the art of speaking and writing effectively that dates back at least as far as ancient Athens in the Western tradition. Aristotle described rhetoric as "the faculty of discovering in any particular case all of the available means of persuasion" and this definition, or similar ones offered by Cicero, Quintilian, Augustine, and others, point to the study of rhetoric as the analysis and use of words to persuade an audience.

The ability to persuade effectively has implications for the use of that power, so some rhetoricians also engaged the idea of *ethics* within or alongside rhetoric. In the Jesuit educational system, there is a tradition called *eloquentia perfecta,* which is speaking (or writing) well for the greater good. As you study, analyze, and effectively use rhetoric, keep in mind that rhetoric, like many tools, can be utilized in both ethical and unethical ways. As you build knowledge and become more aware of rhetoric in the world around you, recall the practices of *reflection* and *discernment* that are also part of the Jesuit tradition—when you make choices about using your rhetorical skills, remember that rhetoric can serve the greater good, or merely be self-serving.

Though we may not be aware of it, we use and encounter rhetoric all the time in our daily lives. You might engage rhetorical means when you try to persuade your roommate to pick up her dirty socks, or convince your parents to support a trip abroad, or write a cover letter to apply for a new job or internship. In each of these situations, you use persuasion to try to convince an audience of your perspective. Conversely, you also encounter rhetoric everyday in magazine or online ads, opinion pieces in the school newspaper, or when you watch political speeches on television or the Internet. Even memes, by using stock images and brief lines of text, provide short arguments that make a claim and try to convince the viewer of a particular perspective.

Because we use and encounter rhetoric so often in our everyday lives, it is important to understand how it operates in order to use it effectively and ethically. It is also crucial to recognize how rhetoric works on *you* in your daily encounters with texts, people, and ideas. With knowledge of how rhetorical appeals work, you will be able to engage the world around you with greater discernment, which will allow you to make more informed choices about the arguments you regularly witness.

Rhetorical Terms and Appeals

In ENGL 101 and 115 you will likely learn about *rhetorical appeals,* or the specific ways that people are generally persuaded. The three main appeals are:

- *Ethos*: The character or authority of the speaker/writer, which includes the reasons you might trust what a particular person says, either because of her virtues or knowledge. Audiences are not persuaded by speakers they do not trust.
- *Logos*: This is the logic or reason behind an argument that appeals to our rationality. An argument has to make sense and be backed with evidence in order for it to be accepted by an audience.
- *Pathos*: The emotions we feel when faced with a situation can also affect our choices and beliefs. We may be moved by compassion or fear to take a certain action for a social cause, or may feel joy and fulfillment when we are convinced to spend the weekend on vacation with friends.

Ideally, all of these appeals will work together in well-constructed, logical arguments that speak to our values and are presented to us by ethical, knowledgeable people. As you can imagine, though, this is not always the case, which is why it is so important to discern and identify rhetorical appeals in our everyday lives.

Other terms you may hear in your studies of rhetoric include:

- *Audience*: All rhetorical acts engage a rhetor and an audience to whom the rhetor speaks or writes. You already tailor your messages depending upon your audience, whether you are aware of it or not. When writing rhetorically, you will make more conscious choices about wording, style, or method of delivery in order to reach your audience most effectively.
- *Purpose*: All communication has a distinct and specific purpose. Do you want your audience to take a particular action? Or believe a new idea? Knowing what you want to accomplish with your writing will help you craft more effective texts.
- *Kairos*: This refers to the timing of a rhetorical text—what is relevant today may no longer make sense three months from now. A rhetorically effective text will take into account the timing of events and will arise at the proper moment.
- *Exigence*: Rhetorical texts arise in response to stimuli or events and may pose a potential solution to a problem. The exigence is a state that demands attention and the rhetorical text is what arises in response to it.
- *The Five Canons of Rhetoric*
  1. *Invention*: Pre-writing work such as brainstorming, heuristics, listing, etc, that allows you to "find" your argument
  2. *Arrangement*: Putting together your argument in a logical, effective way that your audience can easily follow
  3. *Style*: May include the wording, tone, or appearance appropriate for your text, audience, and purpose

4. *Memory*: In classical rhetoric, this refers to memorizing a speech, but today it can indicate referencing citations, digital memory, or public/cultural memory that influences rhetorical texts
5. *Delivery*: For classic oratory, this might include gestures or tone of voice, but in written texts may refer to the way writing is presented on a page, digital delivery, or forms such as video or podcasts

Knowing these terms and understanding their application will give you a vocabulary to analyze, think, and write about the way rhetoric works. In ENGL 101 and 115 you will likely conduct a *rhetorical analysis* at some point, which will ask you to examine a text and analyze its rhetorical components. You may also be asked to consciously utilize rhetorical appeals in your own writing as a means of creating more effective arguments. These may be new genres of writing, and examples of effective rhetorical analyses and rhetorically grounded arguments will be offered later in this book.

Though you may not have realized it, you are already surrounded by rhetoric and confront rhetorical appeals everyday. By understanding how rhetoric operates, you will be able to identify the persuasive tactics you encounter in order to make more informed choices *and* to interrogate your own use of rhetoric to ensure that your rhetorical skills are used in a way that serves your values.

Research, Citation, and Academic Honesty

In college, you will be asked to write research papers in many of your classes. In ENGL 101 and 115, you will learn about the conventions of research and citation as part of your course work. Again, some of this may be review, but many students find that college-level research writing entails more careful documentation than their high school writing required.

Research can be viewed as an ongoing conversation between multiple parties within and across disciplines. As new ideas are discovered, academics write up their findings and publish them in scholarly journals, where they are reviewed by their peers. When you read scholarly articles, you are "listening" to those conversations, and when you write research papers you are "joining" that conversation by synthesizing information and applying it to your own interests.

One way that you can start to understand and analyze this scholarly conversation more thoroughly is through creating an Annotated Bibliography as part of your research work. Although what is expected for this assignment will vary depending upon the course, discipline, parameters of the upcoming paper you may write, concepts covered in class, or the preferences of your professor, all annotated bibliographies serve the purpose of both *summarizing* and *analyzing* the specific sources you are exploring in your research process. In addition to demonstrating to your professor that you are actively engaging with research on your topic, creating an annotated bibliography also allows you to contemplate sources more deeply, analyze their position or content, and consider how each source contributes to the work you are doing yourself. This thinking and writing process can be very beneficial to you as you conduct research, allowing you to pause and think critically about each source that you examine prior to using it in a research paper or other assignment.

For an assignment like this, you would list each source alphabetically by author in proper citation format (MLA for English classes, but check with your professor if you are unsure or if you are working on an assignment in a different discipline), and then provide the annotation—a summary and analysis of the source—underneath the entry. If you receive an Annotated Bibliography as an assignment, be sure to check with your professor about what he or she expects to see in each entry and how it should be formatted, as this can vary greatly depending upon the course. Remember, too, that this is something you can take to the Writing Center for additional feedback or help with citation methods.

Because scholarly writing depends so much on the ongoing research "conversation," the academic community has very high standards for crediting and citing research that others have conducted. While standards for citing and incorporating sources into your own work may vary in high school, once you are in college, there are particular rules that you must follow in order to keep your writing and research practices ethical.

In college, you will likely be asked to integrate outside research with your own ideas. When you do this, you may make claims or express ideas that are yours, and then back them up with evidence that comes from outside sources. This is a more complicated process than, say, writing a research report that summarizes the ideas of someone else, or an opinion paper that simply expresses your own position. In college writing, you will often be asked to integrate both of these ideas into a more complex written argument.

When you utilize research conducted by others, it is important to always attribute those ideas to their sources. There are a variety of ways that you might incorporate outside sources into your work, including:

- *Quotes*: a short passage that is written out word for word exactly as the original author stated it
- *Paraphrase*: a segment of someone else's work that you have put into your own words
- *Summary*: condensing the overall idea of a work into a much shorter format in your own words

To maintain academic honesty you must cite the sources you use in all three of these cases.

Citing a source typically includes in-text citations inside of parentheses at the end of the sentence where the outside source is quoted, paraphrased, or summarized. For MLA format, which you will use in most of your English classes, this will include the author's last name and the page number of the article or book where you found the information. Your papers should always include a Works Cited page, where you list all of the sources you used for your paper, arranged alphabetically by the author's last name; this should also include important publishing information, which will be covered in your class or found in an MLA style guide.

Please note that as of March 2016 MLA has moved to 8th edition style guidelines, so the information in your textbook may not be updated if you are using an edition published prior to that time. You may need to consult an online database such as Purdue Owl, or purchase an MLA update supplement for your textbook.

Your ENGL 101 or 115 instructor will go over proper citation formats in class for different types of documents, but the first and most important step is to remember that you *must cite these sources,* even if you do not quote them directly. Although you may lose points for formatting a citation incorrectly or need to revise if you've made a mistake, citing outside work in the first place will allow you to avoid charges of plagiarism or academic dishonesty, which are much more serious.

Avoiding Plagiarism

Plagiarism can be defined as using someone else's words or ideas without properly identifying the source. Plagiarism can carry dire consequences for students who engage in it, including failing grades for the assignment or course, and in some cases, suspension[1]. Here are some basic types of plagiarism that can compromise a student's academic integrity:

- *Intentional Misrepresentation:* This occurs when a student deliberately attempts to present another's work as his or her own. This can include copying or paraphrasing someone else's writing without attributing the source, buying a paper online, or having someone else write the paper.
- *Self-Plagiarism*: This type of misrepresentation happens when a student "recycles" a paper written previously for another class or context. In some cases, you may want to continue research that you have conducted for another class or project, but *you may not use any writing that you have already turned in* for a grade. If you decide to further previous research, it is best to check with your instructor and be totally honest about what you are doing so that your motives and writing process are completely transparent.
- *Unintentional Misrepresentation:* When a student is not familiar with community citation standards, or that these standards may be different from what you did in high school, it is possible to plagiarize due to uncertainty or lack of knowledge. When in doubt, cite your sources.
- *Patchwriting*: Rebecca Moore Howard (1993) defines "patchwriting" as *"copying from a source text and then deleting some words, altering grammatical structures, or plugging in one-for-one synonym-substitutes."* This type of plagiarism is not always the result of dishonesty; sometimes it occurs because students are not familiar with the ideas or language they are attempting to incorporate. Nevertheless, it is still considered plagiarism *even if the sources are cited.*

1 For more information about the penalties for academic dishonesty, see: http://www.xavier.edu/library/xu-tutor/Xaviers-Policy-on-Academic-Honesty.cfm

- *Excessive Quotation*: Even if you cite your sources, you cannot cobble together a paper based mostly upon the words or ideas of others. When you use long quotes, do so sparingly and only when the author has stated an idea in such a way that it warrants the in-depth use of another's specific words. (Also check MLA citation guidelines, as long quotes require block formatting that is different from short quotes.) Be wary, however, about using multiple sets of long quotes as this may border on plagiarism, even if you cite the sources. When you write papers in college, the bulk of the words and ideas should be your own.

In some cases, you may not need to cite a source. For instance, when referring to your own personal experiences or thoughts, original research you have conducted yourself, or when you use common knowledge or widely accepted facts, a source is not necessary. What constitutes "common knowledge" may vary widely, but is generally considered to be a fact that is easily accessible and consistent across many sources (e.g. the Declaration of Independence was ratified in 1776). However, if you are not sure if your information is considered common knowledge, *cite the source*.

Integrating sources correctly into your own work will also help you to avoid plagiarism, as doing so allows you to clearly show in your writing which ideas are your own and which ideas come from others. Although you may understand how a source supports or more fully clarifies your own work, it is important to explicitly explain that to your audience. Framing outside information will make your work more effective and also help you avoid accidental plagiarism:

- *Introduce* the integrated work with a short sentence or phrase that contextualizes the information for your reader.
- *Quote, Paraphrase, or Summarize* the work, including proper in-text documentation per citation style and be sure to include all sources used in your Works Cited page.
- *Comment* on the work and how it relates to the argument or information you are presenting. This will help your reader understand how you interpret the work you are citing and its relationship to your own ideas.

Learning to effectively and ethically integrate research into your own writing is a key component of what you will learn in ENGL 101 and 115, skills that will also support your success in other classes throughout your time as a student. While other disciplines may use different citation styles (such as APA or Chicago) all disciplines value honest, ethical research practices and eschew anything that could be construed as plagiarism or misappropriation of another's work. For these reasons, it is very important that you learn and understand the research and citation methods expected of you in college, as the consequences for not following these community standards can be dire, with long-term effects on your academic career.

Consequences for Academic Dishonesty

Your instructor will have a clearly stated plagiarism policy in your ENGL 101 or 115 syllabus and you should be very clear about the possible ramifications for not properly attributing your sources. Plagiarism often occurs when a student is pressed for time or overwhelmed by an assignment; sometimes, an otherwise honest student may make unfortunate choices in high pressure situations that lead to more work, trouble, and upset than taking the time to do the work honestly. If you find yourself in a situation where you are stuck or afraid that you cannot complete the work on time, talk to your instructor, or take your assignment prompt to the Writing Center for help or clarification. Even requesting an extension or having points docked for turning in a paper late are much less severe than a charge of plagiarism.

Students can mistakenly believe that their instructors will not know if they have plagiarized or copied a paper—in full or in part—from another source, but this is rarely the case. Software such as Turnitin catches many cases of plagiarism and instructors generally know the writing styles of their students. With Internet technology, it is very easy for instructors to search for key terms in their students' work to see if a paper has been plagiarized or recycled from another source. Even under situations of stress, it is never a good idea to turn in work that is not fully your own—an honestly but poorly written draft can be corrected and recovered from, whereas an academic dishonesty charge will follow you throughout your college career.

Xavier's Academic Honesty Policy States:

The pursuit of truth demands high standards of personal honesty. Academic and professional life requires a trust based upon integrity of the written and spoken word. Accordingly, violations of certain standards of ethical behavior will not be tolerated at Xavier University. These include theft, cheating, plagiarism, unauthorized assistance in assignments and tests, unauthorized copying of computer software, the falsification of results and material submitted in reports or admission and registration documents, and the falsification of any academic record including letters of recommendation.

All work submitted for academic evaluation must be the student's own. Certainly, the activities of other scholars will influence all students. However, the direct and unattributed use of another's efforts is prohibited as is the use of any work untruthfully submitted as one's own.

Penalties for violations of this policy may include one or more of the following: a zero for that assignment or test, an "F" in the course, and expulsion from the University. The dean of the college in which the student is enrolled is to be informed in writing of all such incidents, though the teacher has full authority to assign the grade for the assignment, test, or course. If disputes of interpretation arise, the student, faculty member, and chair should attempt to resolve the difficulty. If this is unsatisfactory, the dean will rule in the matter. As a final appeal, the academic vice president will call a committee of tenured faculty for the purpose of making a final determination.

Please note that, not only are there immediate consequences for academic dishonesty (including a zero for the assignment, an "F" for the course, or expulsion from the University), but also that this action will be reported to the Dean's office of the college in which you are enrolled, and that a record of this action will be recorded. While the ramifications for *any* instance of academic dishonesty are definitely not worth the risk, in the case of a second or repeated offense, the consequences are typically much more severe.

In all cases, academic honesty and integrity are always the "write path" to take. Citing your sources clearly and integrating them effectively into your own work will make you a better writer *and* help ensure your acceptance into a community of scholars.

Resources for Students

Xavier University McDonald Memorial Library

We often think of the library as a place to go to find books, but the library actually offers many more services that will be of use to you as you research various projects. In addition to the books housed in the library, you can also use OhioLINK or Inter-Library Loan (ILL) to check out any book available in libraries across the state or country. This gives you access to many more books than could be contained in a single building on campus. Keep in mind, though, that these services may take a few days to process your request and get the book to Xavier for you to pick up, so always start your research process early.

In addition to traditional print books, the library offers services to connect Xavier students to a variety of journals, media, and other resources. By using Search @ XU, you can easily access thousands of resources. In ENGL 101 or 115, your class may take a trip to the library, or a librarian may come to your class to talk with you about how to search the databases and find the information you need. You can also drop by the library, connect via chat text, or email the librarians to ask questions or to seek help if you are having trouble finding information.

The library has a makerspace on the first floor, right as you come in the main entrance from the Academic Mall. The makerspace is open to all students to explore, design, create, build, and collaborate using technologies such as 3D printing and 3D scanning, robotics, circuitry, programming, a laser etcher and CNC mill, tools, crafts, and more.

In addition to the library services, you can also use the Conaton Learning Commons (connected to the library building) as a place to study or meet with classmates to work on group projects. There are fourteen group study rooms in the CLC with capacities that range from two or three people, up to ten people. Many of these rooms are equipped with white boards or plasma screen projectors with web access, so you can easily share your work and collaborate in these spaces. There are also two small computing labs with access to photocopiers, printers, scanners, and computer workstations. Other student support services in the Conaton Learning Commons include the Learning Assistance Center,

Math Lab, Writing Center, Language Resource Center, Academic Advising, and the Digital Media Lab. All of these services are here for you to use and can help support your writing and research in a variety of courses.

James A. Glenn Writing Center

The Writing Center is another important resource for students at Xavier to help them develop writing skills and to support them with writing assignments in various classes. Located in the CLC 400 (overlooking the circulation desk), the Writing Center offers peer tutoring help with writing during any part of the drafting process. While this is a great place to come if you want someone else to look over your paper once you have a rough draft, the Writing Center tutors can also help you understand an assignment more fully before you start drafting, work with brainstorming ideas, give assistance organizing a paper, offer direction if you are halfway through an essay and get stuck, or provide information about documenting sources. At any stage of the drafting process, the Writing Center is an invaluable asset for students working on writing.

If you use the Writing Center, it is best to make an appointment in advance by calling (513-745-2875), since there may or may not be a tutor available if you just walk in. While most students go to the Writing Center in person, sessions can also be conducted via Skype or email at writingcenter@xavier.edu.

When you go, be prepared with your assignment prompt, and name of the class and professor, as well as any notes, texts that your writing refers to, and drafts or outlines you have already done. Think about areas where you need the most help with the assignment and have questions ready to ask the tutor, as this will allow you to make the best use of your time. It is optimal to plan to go to the Writing Center a few days before an assignment is due so that you have time to make revisions, or even do additional research, before turning in your work for your class. Sessions last about fifty minutes and the Writing Center is open a variety of hours (including Sundays) so that it is possible to find time in your schedule to make an appointment.

Some students mistakenly believe that the Writing Center is only used by people who struggle with writing or who are "bad" writers. The truth is, no matter how skilled a writer you are, receiving feedback on what you have written can improve the overall quality of the work you turn in. Everyone benefits from having reviews of their writing and almost all writing can be developed more fully. The Writing Center is a key support service for success in ENGL 101 and 115, as well as other courses and projects that require writing. Be sure to utilize this resource while you are at Xavier.

Some Words About Success

In your first year at Xavier, you will be building the skills you need to succeed in your classes, as well as your life beyond the university. The writing you will practice in your ENGL 101 and 115 courses is a part of that skillset, but it does not exist in isolation. Part of success in writing—or college, or life in general—is planning your time wisely so that you are able to meet all of your commitments without being overwhelmed or stressed in the process. It may be a change for you to have to plan so many activities, assignments, and classes yourself, but learning to do so effectively will ensure that you are able to be successful in your courses.

Learning to write well takes practice, which is why we promote a process-based approach to writing. You may find writing more challenging in college than you did in high school, but as with learning any new skill, you will find that you develop efficacy the more you practice. Be sure to give yourself enough time to work on your writing assignments, even in courses where the process itself is not emphasized as much as it is in ENGL 101 or 115. Brainstorm, jot down outlines, take good notes on your research, write rough drafts, and visit the Writing Center. All of these practices will not only increase the likelihood of achieving higher grades on your papers, but also develop the skills you need to write well in all areas of your life.

Remember though, as with any skill, writing capability is acquired over time and with repeated practice. While feedback from peers, your professor, or a peer tutor can aid in developing your skills as a writer, these practices do not automatically guarantee that you will get the highest grade possible on an assignment. All students build competency over time, and peers, professors, and tutors can only address a few issues at once. Be patient with the process and engage all of the resources available to you at Xavier to ensure that you reach the highest level of writing success you can during your time in college.

Student Work

How to Use This Text

In the upcoming pages, you will find examples of student work from first year students who, just like you, took ENGL 101 and/or 115. These examples can be used in a variety of ways and are here to support the writing that you will do in your first year at Xavier.

One way that these student essays can help you is to illustrate what the different genres of writing you may encounter in ENGL 101 and 115 look like. It can be hard to craft a particular kind of writing, such as a rhetorical analysis or ethnography, if you have no idea what these genres are or should include. By looking at an example paper, you can see what typically goes into writing this type of paper, as well as observe how this can be done particularly well.

These papers do not serve as a rigid template for you to copy. Rather, you should use these texts as models for what to expect in a particular genre of writing, what you should include, what "works" about a piece of writing, and then consider how you can adapt or include those skills in your own work. By "stepping back" from a text and asking questions about how it is composed, you can analyze not only the content, but also the rhetorical and compositional strategies that are employed in creating that piece of writing.

To guide you through reading these examples, each paper will be foregrounded by a reflection from the students themselves, discussing their writing process for that paper. You can see through their words what challenges, obstacles, strategies, and steps they took to get to the finished piece of writing that is published in this book. As readers, we often only get to see the product of a writer's efforts, but in this text, you will also gain insight about the process that led to these essays. By reading these reflections by students, you might find that you relate to some of their struggles, or learn an important tip that could help you with your own writing.

After the reflection you will find the essay itself, followed by a short series of questions. These questions ask you to look more deeply at the writing itself, to ascertain what you think the writer was doing or intending at different points along the way. How does this writer transition from one idea to the next? What kinds of sources does this writer use as support for her argument? How are quotes integrated into this argument? These are the kinds of questions that may be presented after the essay itself, for you to consider and/or for your instructor to use in class to prompt discussion about the writing process.

By examining the writing of other students who were working under similar conditions, you can seek guidance and encouragement for your own work in first year composition and rhetoric courses at Xavier. Additionally, by analyzing the writing process in this way, you can learn more about the way that you write. How do *you* transition between ideas? Support your claims? Or integrate quotes? By getting into the habit of analyzing writing itself, rather than only its content, you gain *meta-cognitive awareness* of your own writing process. By understanding how writing happens, you can acquire insight about what you do, how you do it, and why.

This knowledge can allow you to make more conscious choices and utilize the Jesuit principles of *reflection* and *discernment*. Through reflection on your writing, you can learn more about yourself as a writer and communicator, and then make more discerning choices about those practices. As you develop your skills as a writer in your first year courses, you will build the foundation of your future academic success, as well as establish tools with which to participate in your communities, careers, and civic lives. This text is designed to assist you in those endeavors and to serve as a guide for your first year as a college writer.

The D'Artagnan Award

The essays that you find in this book all come from entries for the D'Artagnan Award, an annual award co-sponsored by Xavier's Writing Program, The Dean's Office, and the Writing Center. Each year, students are encouraged to submit their best work from ENGL 101 and 115 for this award. The submitted essays can be written in any genre and the top three winners, along with a selection of other exemplary student work, will be published in *The Write Path: First Year Composition and Rhetoric at Xavier* for the following year.

The name for this award was chosen specifically because D'Artagnan, like our first year writers, had to work hard to improve his skills, overcome obstacles, and rise to the challenge of new situations that require maturity and development. First year students who win this award become leaders for future students, as their work will become a tool to guide new first year writers on their educational journey.

As you use this text this year and develop your writing skills in ENGL 101 and 115, please consider submitting your favorite pieces for next year's D'Artagnan Award. You can learn more about this award and submit work anytime throughout the year at: http://www.xavier.edu/english-department/The-DArtagnan-Award.cfm.

D'Artagnan Award Winners
Category: Research-Based Argument

This year's top three winners for the D'Artagnan Award all happen to fall into the category of research-based argument. While in future years these three award-winning essays may be comprised of different genres, for this year the First Place winner, First Runner Up, and Second Runner Up are all research-based arguments of one kind or another.

Our First Place essay, "A Societal Attempt to Find Order in Murder" by Ellen Siefke, was written for her ENGL 115 course and explores questions about why crime shows are so popular. Our editorial team chose this as the winning essay because it demonstrates how a student might take an idea or question and use that as a starting point for research. Her original question ("Why are people fascinated with depictions of murder in crime shows?") might be viewed as rather abstract, but to illustrate her point, Ellen utilizes concrete examples to show her reader exactly what she means. In fact, her thesis is a series of questions, which highlights the inquiry-based approach she used in her research, and also serves to pull readers into her essay by inviting them to ask these same questions of themselves. The editorial board also appreciated how Ellen arranged and organized her argument, which incorporates many different sources along with the various primary texts she analyzed to form her argument. Within her essay, she questions important ideas that are fundamental to the way we think about morality, life, death, values, and culture, and she does so in a way that makes readers more aware of their own behavior and assumptions. Her sophisticated use of sources and critical thinking skills made this essay interesting and memorable, qualities that are very effective when crafting arguments.

The First Runner Up award goes to David Dreier, for his essay entitled "Shoot First, Stay Alive to Ask Questions Later," which explores the common assumption that viewers have of "heroes," who only shoot if someone else fires first. Like Ellen, David approaches his topic in a very inquiry-based fashion, asking important questions about where the line is drawn between heroes, villains, and anti-heroes, though more specifically, he narrows down his focus to question the criteria we have for when it is acceptable for a hero to kill someone. In his essay, he begins by illustrating his point using a concrete example that many readers will recognize: a scene from *Star Wars,* which was later edited so that Han Solo does not appear to shoot first when threatened by a bounty hunter. David focuses on particular movies where what is deemed "heroic" is somewhat ambiguous and argues that sometimes killing in a movie is necessary. The editorial team was impressed by David's use of multiple examples from films to illustrate his point and show the reader exactly the issues he was trying to elucidate. David also actively engages with a variety of sources, including scholarly works, in order to round out his argument. David's essay encourages readers to think more deeply about their expectations for what is considered "heroic," and while he focuses on analyzing movies for this paper, these questions easily extend beyond the realm of entertainment.

Stephen Bothwell is our Second Runner Up winner with his essay "Stress: Not Just a Matter of Time," which argues that the demands of being a college student lead to unhealthy levels of stress for many. Unlike the previous two arguments, Stephen's piece is a causal essay, where he is positing, not just that this condition exists, but rather that it is *caused* by a particular set of conditions unique to college students. Because a causal argument seeks to show causality, the arrangement of the evidence is particularly important in order for the claim to be effective. The editorial team thought that Stephen made effective choices in the way he organized and presented his evidence to readers to make his assertions convincing. Additionally, the editorial team was impressed by the way he integrated and used sources so that his research supports his argument without overpowering it. He begins his essay by drawing readers in, painting a vivid, relatable image of the stress experienced by many college students. This contrasts to, and connects effectively with, his ample use of facts and statistics, which conclusively demonstrate that stress is a real problem for college students, largely due to the particular exigencies of life at the university. His essay is focused squarely on a genuine issue that is of importance to his audience, and he calls for measures to alleviate stress when it becomes unhealthy.

Although you may find that your classes require you to write different types of research-based arguments, or that your prompts are very different from the ones for which these essays were written, there are elements you will see in these three research-based arguments that will help you with your assignments. When reading these essays, notice how the writer sets up his or her argument. Is it engaging to the reader? What kinds of evidence do these writers use? How are sources integrated? Think, too, about how papers begin and end. What draws a reader into a paper? How do papers conclude in a way that is memorable and effective? Each of these three papers offers in-depth arguments that rely upon quite a bit of information. Notice how the arguments are arranged. What claims come first, second, and third? Is the order effective? Why might the author have chosen to set up the argument in this manner?

In all three cases, these students have produced exemplary work in their first year writing courses and learned skills for research writing and argumentation that will serve them in other courses. Although each discipline has its own sets of rules and expectations for writing, many of these skills—such as integrating sources, making claims, using evidence to support one's position, etc.—will be necessary in a variety of contexts. Your first year writing courses will help you develop these skills more fully so that you are able to utilize them effectively throughout your time at Xavier.

In the following student selections, you will read reflections from Ellen, David, and Stephen before reading their work. This will give you insight about the different processes that produced these pieces and offer advice from these writers that may help you in your own writing process. At the end of each essay, you will find questions to consider about the particular piece you have just completed reading. These prompts will guide you to explore the writing and rhetorical strategies used by these student writers so that you might gain deeper understanding of what makes this work effective.

The editorial team hopes that you enjoy reading these essays as much as we did and that you, too, are able to develop your writing, argument, and research skills in your first year at Xavier.

A Societal Attempt to Find Order in Murder

Ellen Siefke
First Place Winner | Research-Based Argument

Reflection

I struggled a bit in figuring out an idea for this paper; I knew that I wanted to research something different, something that did not involve politics, the environment, or any other hot-button issues. After discussion with peers, I decided to investigate a longtime curiosity of mine regarding the popularity of crime shows. To be honest, I had no idea if it even would prove a viable topic and mentioned my uncertainty to my rhetoric professor. She replied that it sounded interesting and urged me to pursue it further. With that encouragement, I took off, and the subsequent five weeks produced this essay.

The most challenging part of this assignment involved the integration of sources. I read many articles, some of them a quick read and others more than 20 pages long. It was especially difficult to determine how to incorporate the information from the longer articles into my essay, so I highlighted or underlined what I deemed the most important lines and then used those in citations. Outside of integration of quotes, another difficulty was finding the right sources. While researching, I would discover seemingly the perfect article only to learn it was exceptionally unhelpful. It is natural to want to go with the first sources you find, but I would advise students to dig a little deeper and to continue to research throughout the writing process. After drafting, for example, I determined a few holes research-wise, but with some digging, I was able to find appropriate sources for them.

In terms of the process itself, my professor proved helpful because she set deadlines for tasks like a research plan, an outline, and a draft. She also very specifically stated what was expected at each step, and these guidelines helped keep me on track. It also greatly improved the revising process, which consisted of my own revisions as well as peer editing sessions in class. Though I did not go to the Writing Center, my instructor commented on our outline and research plan. Even if a professor does not set specific deadlines for having a certain amount done, I would heavily recommend creating a plan of sorts—one that states, for example, that by this Friday, I will have completed all of my preliminary research. It really does help keep you on track and keeps the stress levels to a minimum. In addition, peer review sessions are extremely helpful because an outside source can provide valuable feedback and offer a different perspective on your topic.

A Societal Attempt to Find Order in Murder

"CSI." "NCIS." "Castle." "Criminal Minds." "Law and Order." "American Psycho." "Silence of the Lambs." "Nightmare on Elm Street." The list of crime media, from movies to TV shows to books, goes on. Normally, the various media follow a systematic formula: bad guy kills some people, the detective team comes to stop the villain, team narrowly misses him, bad guy implements a larger plot, only to be stopped in the nick of time by the good guys. Somehow, though, this formula resonates with audiences who keep tuning in for more. A curious observer of this phenomenon, however, might note that the formula does not stray from rather horrific crimes. "Criminal Minds" alone has covered ritualistic killings, savage burnings, and terrifying kidnappings, among others. Normally, people feel repulsed by this and avoid such appalling stories. So why does putting them on a screen suddenly reverse the repulsion? What makes a Jack the Ripper-esque figure sickening in real life but fascinating on TV? What makes a character like Dexter, a cop by day and full-blown serial killer by night, so appealing when any real-life persona would draw outrage?

Part of the answer lies in our very nature as human beings to classify our world in a black-and-white manner, especially when it comes to issues of morality and ethics. According to Ashley M. Donnelly's article in *The Journal of Popular Culture,* "American popular culture typically struggles with the idea of a lack of a moral center" (17). Not having an established moral center creates chaos and confusion and leans toward relativist thinking, in which each person has his/her own set of morals without any truth in morality. The relativist viewpoint assumes a natural sense of chaos where it is impossible to clearly define any set of morals or values, the very notion with which Donnelly claims Americans struggle. Therefore, we create a sense of normalcy and label anything falling outside that sphere as "abnormal," distinguishing instantly between those who conform to societal norms and those who stray from them (Donnelly 17). Since our minds tend toward simplistic thinking, we prefer this quick way of separating ourselves from the killers instead of having to deal with complicated issues of morality. According to a five-decade long study conducted by Daniel Kahneman, a Nobel Laureate and Princeton psychology professor, people use mental shortcuts when facing a difficult or complicated decision to avoid delving too deeply into an issue (Lehrer). Jonah Lehrer, who wrote about Kahneman's work in *The New Yorker,* explains that "these shortcuts aren't a faster way of doing the math; they're a way of skipping the math altogether" (Lehrer). Though Kahneman's study did not specifically focus on serial killer culture, his findings can easily be applied to the subject. To dive into the mind of a serial killer can prove physically and mentally exhausting and reflect poorly on us as a society, so if we can just label the murderer as "other" and let the matter rest, we will. To determine why exactly a particular person falls outside our sphere of normalcy would be far too strenuous for our tastes, so we prefer to make a snap judgment and move on. Labeling Sandy Hook shooter Adam Lanza or Aurora movie theater shooter James Holmes as "different" rather than trying to determine why they killed so many people is much simpler and avoids the messy task of using psychology and fancy terms about the brain. This all-or-nothing concept of morality allows us to avoid the tough gray area of ethics and simply say a person is either with us or against us (Donnelly 21).

Crime media takes full advantage of this notion and structures plotlines to revolve around our need for a system of quick identification. We can readily point out the criminals and killers in a TV show because they differ from us in obvious manners—they often lack social graces, exhibit odd habits, and generally emit a creepy vibe. TV shows simplify the idea of a serial killer and boil it down to "he's not like the rest of us" (Donnelly 18). For example, a major villain in the "Criminal Minds" series is the Reaper, who antagonizes the BAU detective team for most of the fifth season; actually named George Foyet, the Reaper is portrayed as a psychotic killing machine, showing no remorse for his actions and never hesitating to slaughter his victims. When viewers see the Reaper, with his Jason Vorhees-like hockey mask and stereotypical black villainous outfit, they can immediately identify him as one of the "bad guys" because he falls outside their perception of the normal.

Crime media also uses oversimplification in portraying villains based on common stereotypes and misconceptions, as highlighted in an FBI study stating that "much of the general public's knowledge concerning serial murder is a product of Hollywood productions" (FBI). The stereotypes most commonly utilized in crime shows are that killers are white males, killers are dysfunctional loners, killers are geniuses, and killers want to get caught and play twisted games with the detective team chasing them. All permeate crime shows, and all contribute to a quasi-romanticized view of serial murder, a view that we as humans readily understand. The stereotypes, by definition, play perfectly into viewers' hands because they reinforce that preferred simplistic thinking—we associate a loner with shady business, a genius with evil acts, a white male with pedophiliac tendencies. Crime shows use plotlines "created to heighten the interest of audiences, rather than to accurately portray serial murder" (FBI), and screenwriters know what their audiences want. It is little surprise, then, that "NCIS" still boasts close to 20 million viewers per episode (*"NCIS"*), "Law and Order: SVU" has hung around since 1999 and is now in its seventeenth season (*"Law and Order"*), and "Bones" remains a staple on FOX (*"Bones"*). Through the use of clear signals and stereotypes, crime shows remain attuned to viewers' wants and allow them to avoid thinking too much on the morbid and graphic themes played out on the screen.

Almost all crime shows, from "NCIS" to "CSI" to "Castle," utilize similar methods. The episodes begin with the murder itself, often accompanied by ominous music: we know what lies ahead and need not think too hard on it. Typical episodes involve the respective detective teams chasing after the killer, being foiled a few times, finally putting all of the clues together, and then triumphantly nabbing the criminal in the nick of time before some larger, more egregious plot can be carried out. Despite this relatively fixed formula, people keep coming back for more. In its peak, "CSI" boasted around 25 million viewers per season (*"CSI"*), which led to the creation of several spinoffs like "CSI: Miami" and "CSI: New York." "Criminal Minds," though never reaching the same popularity as "CSI," continues to see around 10 million viewers per episode and has maintained its Wednesday night primetime spot (*"Criminal Minds"*). Clearly, though the episodes show little variety in their structure, they resonate with audiences. But is it enough to attribute this popularity merely to the human tendency to oversimplify? At the end of the day, crime shows are still about crime and murder, a rather taboo and grisly subject, so there must be other forces at work here.

Table 1 The chart below displays the viewership statistics for the fifteenth and final season of "CSI." Despite being on the air for around fifteen years, the show still had close to 10 million viewers per episode (*"CSI"*).

Air Date		Episode	18–49 Demo	% Demo Change	Viewers (Mil)	% Million Change
Sunday	09/28/2014	15-01	1.40	–30.00%†	9.410	2.63%†
Sunday	10/05/2014	15-02	1.30	–7.14%	8.092	–14.01%
Sunday	10/12/2014	15-03	1.36	4.62%	8.771	8.39%
Sunday	10/19/2014	15-04	1.37	0.74%	8.855	0.96%
Sunday	11/09/2014	15-05	1.24	–9.49%	8.669	–2.10%
Sunday	11/16/2014	15-06	1.29	4.03%	8.447	–2.56%
Sunday	11/23/2014	15-07	1.28	–0.78%	7.877	–6.75%
Sunday	11/30/2014	15-08	1.38	7.81%	8.303	5.41%
Sunday	12/07/2014	15-09	1.24	–10.14%	7.887	–5.01%
Sunday	12/14/2014	15-10	1.23	–0.81%	7.475	–5.22%
Sunday	12/21/2014	15-11	1.29	4.88%	7.340	–1.81%
Sunday	12/28/2014	15-12	1.44	11.63%	7.842	6.84%
Sunday	01/04/2015	15-13	1.27	–11.81%	8.617	9.88%
Sunday	01/25/2015	15-14	1.20	–5.51%	8.251	–4.25%
Sunday	01/25/2015	15-15	1.28	6.69%	8.297	0.56%
Tuesday	01/27/2015	15-16	1.60	25.00%	10.377	25.07%
Sunday	02/15/2015	15-17	1.12	–30.00%	7.116	–31.43%
Sunday	02/15/2015	15-18	1.08	–3.57%	7.119	0.04%

The other major reason that we indulge in crime shows is that they reinforce our own moral codes and values and confirm that they still function. Donnelly asserts that "our recognized acceptance of the Other must further perpetuate our ideologies" (23). We like to watch crime shows for their formulaic plot that always allows the good guys to win—even if we must wait the entire season, a common technique used by writers to build suspense and maintain viewership. Donnelly uses the example of anti-heroes to illustrate this point; she specifically looks to Henry from "Henry: Portrait of a Serial Killer," John McNaughton's 1986 psychological thriller that depicts the titular character as he embarks on a cross-country killing spree, randomly slaying his victims. Donnelly claims that these types of characters, who kill seemingly for no reason, "[give] us something real to fear within our own society" (20). This fear is the fear of darkness within ourselves—in the case of Henry, there exists no apparent external cause for evil other than the menacing presence of it. The popular crime villain, however, always has a clear *modus operandi,* or method of killing, a clear motive, and a clear reason for resorting to killing, usually in the form of some childhood trauma or bizarre mental disorder. We as viewers process a simplistic reason for the actions played out on screen and are able to push that fear of evil aside. After all, those who are committing the crime are doing so because they are not like us.

The fear of evil about which Donnelly wrote does not exist without warrant; one need only look at the events that have transpired during the course of current young adults' and teenagers' lifetimes. Most young people can hardly remember a pre-9/11 world in which terrorist attacks were hardly on anyone's mind. Not only did the World Trade Center attacks radically alter Americans' sense of privacy and security, but it also, in many ways, set the tone for the years of violence that would follow. We, the upcoming generation, cannot recall any time in which America was not shipping troops off to some Middle Eastern country to fight terrorism. We have no memories of going to an airport and not being subjected to intense scrutiny, all in the name of security and protection. We have never known a world in which we did not constantly hear about the potential dangers from other countries and terrorists or witnessed such horrific attacks as the most recent slaughter in Paris.

The 9/11 attacks are unfortunately far from the only violent event that young adults have experienced. From Virginia Tech in 2007 to Sandy Hook in 2012 to Umpqua Community College in 2015, school shootings have practically become expected. We have heard about so many that they hardly faze us anymore. The recent stories centering on racial tensions, especially involving police brutality, have permeated media outlets, letting us know just how corrupt and decrepit our so-called protectors are. From Ferguson to Freddie Gray, it seems as though the battle is white cops versus black citizens. Each incident increases the tension a little more, and with movements like #BlackLivesMatter, the unrest is unlikely to cease. We are bombarded with messages and stories about how the dangers and increasing violence of contact sports like football and how barbaric they make us seem. Numerous former professional players have sued organizations like the NFL on the grounds that though information about the dangers of concussions, among other injuries, was known, nothing was done in terms of prevention. We constantly read about the latest incidents of gang violence in impoverished inner city neighborhoods, to the point that, for a person living in the Chicagoland area, the body count remains merely a statistic. Suicide and mental illness, as well as addiction stories, permeate the news. Phillip Seymour Hoffman, Heath Ledger, Cory Monteith, and many others gone too soon spread awareness of such severe and debilitating problems and show their true, horrible effects. We are also the anti-bullying generation, practically raised on anti-bullying videos and presentations and movies, so much so that for some, the word "bullying" has ceased to have meaning. All in all, the events of our lives have left us fairly disenfranchised and skeptical regarding the supposed greatness of our country and society. We feel extremely pessimistic about society's ability to function.

Many argue that such events and the prevalence of crime shows and graphic media has left us desensitized to violence and that we no longer feel so strongly about the aforementioned incidents and themes. Surveys like that of the 2011 Red Cross study concerning the post-9/11 attitudes of youth are used to demonstrate our alleged lack of awareness of violence. That study in particular concerned the Geneva Convention, a series of treaties regarding treatment of prisoners and civilians during wartime, and found a lack of understanding surrounding the various humanitarian laws. For example, the study found that forty-eight percent of the youth had never even heard of the Geneva Conventions and otherwise discovered a significant lack of understanding about the treaties (Rose). Proponents of this argument contend that because of our constant exposure to violence, we are more violent people and thus enjoy viewing violent acts.

Another common argument is that our generation's consumption of crime media reflects our materialistic culture and that to us, crime shows represent only one aspect of the "violence of consumerism," as Loughborough University professor Brian Jarvis calls it. Jarvis' article, "Monsters Inc.: Serial Killers and Consumer Culture," claims that the "dreams of the serial killer and the serial consumer converge: reinventing the self through bodily transformation and transcendence" (334). As a generation incessantly deemed materialistic and shallow, we continually seek to fill some sort of void in our lives through spending in the same way a serial killer attempts to fill that same void through slaughter. Therefore, in a sick and twisted way, we can at least empathize with the killers portrayed in crime media, as some small part of us understands the need to feel like we belong, like we have a purpose, like we have worth. The bombardment of celebrity images brandishing perfect bodies and even more perfect style attributes to our lowered feelings of self-worth, so the commercial serial killer's capacity to go above and beyond to feel better parallels our own actions intended for the same effect (336). Thus, while watching crime shows, we see the need to fill the void played out in such a horrific way that we can reconcile with our own need for consumption.

However, these arguments incorrectly assume that young adults want more violence and that we subject ourselves to crime shows to fulfill some hollowness. This could not be further from the truth. We are so battered from all the violence in our lives and from the constant bashing at the hands of society that we just want a break. We just want something, anything, that will tell us we are not going to become bad guys, that the values we have been taught since birth still have some meaning. We are not desensitized; we are exhausted. Crime shows allow us, even for a little while, to pretend that that the world still goes round. Seeing the bad guy get caught and brought to justice time after time again reassures us that no matter what may be happening around us, someone will always be there to save the day, and that our morals and values still have meaning. Watching the detective teams nab the killers reminds us that all hope is not gone and that somehow, our perceptions of right and wrong can still work, even if only on the screen.

Ultimately, our obsession with serial killers speaks to our incessant need to have our values and order confirmed. Christina Gregoriou, an English lecturer at Leeds University, asserts that crime fiction and media "confront us with justice system inadequacies, and demonstrate how we go about understanding good and evil" (284). These shows serve as a way for us to face our own fears about good and evil; they allow us to attribute it to some external force instead of pondering the possibility of its presence within ourselves. With so many examples of evil in recent years, one could hardly blame society, especially young people, for trying to find a way to cope—our indoctrination of violence indicates that our present system of values, a system that we have relied on for as long as we can remember, may not work anymore, and we need something, anything, to assure us that we are all right. Crime fiction gives us an outlet of assurance, a sense of comfort, and a reaffirmation that we possess the proper morals and values that allow us to function as a healthy and "good" society.

Works Cited

"*Bones:* Season 11 Ratings." TV Series Finale, 13 November 2015. Web. 13 November 2015. <http://tvseriesfinale.com/tv-show/bones-season-11-ratings-38292/>

"*Criminal Minds:* Season 11 Ratings." TV Series Finale, 12 November 2015. Web. 13 November 2015. <http://tvseriesfinale.com/tv-show/criminal-minds-season-11-ratings-38269/>

"*CSI*: Season 15 Ratings." TV Series Finale, 13 May 2015. Web. 19 Oct. 2015. <http://tvseriesfinale.com/tv-show/csi-season-15-ratings-34127>

Donnelly, Ashley M. "The New American Hero: Dexter, Serial Killer for the Masses." *The Journal of Popular Culture*. 1 Nov. 2012: 15–26. Web. 21 Oct. 2015.

FBI. "Common Myths and Misconceptions Regarding Serial Murder." *Bedford Book of Genres: A Guide*. Ed. Amy Brazilier and Elizabeth Kleinfeld. Boston: Bedford/St. Martin's, 2013. Web.

Gregoriou, Christiana. "'Times Like These, I Wish There Was a Real Dexter': Unpacking Serial Murder Ideologies and Metaphors from TV's Dexter Internet Forum." *Language and Literature*. 2012: 215–285. Web. 20 Oct. 2015.

Jarvis, Brian. "Monsters Inc.: Serial killers and Consumer Culture." *Crime, Media, Culture: An International Volume*. December 2007: 326–344. Web. 23 October 2015.

"*Law and Order: Special Victims Unit*: Season 17 Ratings." TV Series Finale, 12 November 2015. Web. 13 November 2015. <http://tvseriesfinale.com/tv-show/law-order-special-victims-unit-season-17-ratings-38127/>

Lehrer, Jonah. "Why Smart People Are Stupid." *The New Yorker*. Advance Publications, 12 June 2012. Web. 29 October 2015. <http://www.newyorker.com/tech/frontal-cortex/why-smart-people-are-stupid>

"*NCIS*: Season 12 Ratings." TV Series Finale, 13 May 2015. Web. 11 November 2015. <http://tvseriesfinale.com/tv-show/ncis-tv-show-cbs-season-12-ratings-34022/>

Rose, Emily. "Bridging the Information Gap: American Youth Perceptions on Torture and Civilian Protection." *Social Education*. 2011: 204–207. Web. 4 November 2015.

Questions to Consider

1. In her reflection, Ellen mentions that she struggled to find the right sources to answer her research questions. When you read her essay, do you find that she has effectively answered her own questions? Do you still have any questions that are left unanswered by the end? What other types of sources might she have sought to more thoroughly answer her research questions?

2. Ellen ends the first paragraph of her paper with a couple of questions, rather than a more conventional thesis. What purpose do these questions serve? Do these questions organize and focus her essay in the way that a thesis *statement* would? Why might she have made this choice and in what contexts could this be the most effective way to introduce a main idea?

3. Ellen's paper deals with many abstract concepts, such as morality, meaning, violence, and evil as represented in concrete texts, such as crime shows. How does she use transitions between paragraphs and ideas to guide the reader through these complex ideas? Does this make her argument easier for you to follow? What other strategies might she have employed to lead readers through her argument?

Shoot First, Stay Alive to Ask Questions Later

David Dreier
First Runner Up Winner | Research-Based Argument

Reflection

The idea for my researched argument paper started as an exploration of the differences between heroes, villains, and antiheroes in fiction. I wanted to pursue something in this direction because I had been thinking, with a bit of displeasure, about the general attitudes that exist towards what counts as an "acceptable" behavior for a hero. When my professor (thankfully) pointed out the fact that this topic was far too broad, I started narrowing down my choices, first by sticking strictly to film—the medium I found to be the most accessible and relatable to myself and my fellow college students, who would be my audience. Next, I ditched the antihero-centric angle that I had planned on pursuing and focused instead on the hero side of things, and it eventually came down to asking, "When is it okay for a hero in a film to kill someone?" As I started reading sources and reacting to them, however, I saw that the conclusions I was drawing were not answering this question. Instead, they were affirming a related statement: "It *is* okay for a hero to kill sometimes." This statement may seem a bit simple, and in fact, my professor thought that it would be too narrow of a topic, but my sources proved to me that this was a position in dire need of defending, and everything fell into place from there. I found that finding and using sources was the most challenging part of this assignment, if only because it required an extreme amount of adaptation. As I mentioned before, my topic had to adapt based on the conclusions I drew from my sources. Additionally, I ended up using far fewer sources than I had imagined, and sources of different types than I had predicted. For example, I spent at least a week surveying my classmates about their opinions towards "justified killing," and no part of this survey ended up in the paper. In terms of sources, this assignment was a lesson in "quality over quantity." Fortunately, my professor required me to annotate a few of the sources, so I was really able to evaluate my sources in this light. What I found was that, sometimes, the quality of a source should be determined by the conclusions that can be drawn from it rather than the author's credentials. For example, one of my sources was a fairly mainstream one (i.e., not scholarly), but it was instrumental in making two of my big points. Granted, I went into a much deeper analysis of the scholarly source that I used, so credentials do have their place.

I would probably not recommend this approach to anyone, but I did not have a complete version of this paper until the day it was due. I had two peer review sessions in class; the first time I brought a paper consisting only of my introduction and my first main point, and the second time I brought one that was missing my final point and conclusion. The comments of my peers were a great help, especially when I was working out the specifics of my topic. As I wrote, my status as my own worst critic became the most useful tool in my arsenal—as soon as I wrote something down, I started thinking of ways to improve it. I never used the Writing Center or went to my professor, but I was never worried about the quality or direction of my writing—I just needed to make sure that the creative process unfolded in an acceptable amount of time. I suppose that is part one of my advice to first year writers: make sure you give yourself time to take your time. I often need the stress of a deadline in order to get things done, but the keyword there is *stress,* and it is just as unpleasant as it sounds. You will feel better and write a better paper if you don't rush. Part two of my advice is to be flexible. Don't handcuff yourself to an idea or plan that doesn't leave room for adjustment. If you're anything like me, the paper you *didn't* expect to write will be way better than the one you *did* expect. Finally, part three is to have *fun* with your writing. It's easier to have fun writing for certain subjects than it is for others, but there is usually some way to inject some life into your work no matter the topic, and this is where taking your time can really come in handy. Write papers that you not only want to write, but that you would want to *read* as well, because if nothing else, your professor is going to read your paper, and he or she is much more likely to be in a good grading mood if your paper is a engaging rather than a chore.

Shoot First, Stay Alive to Ask Questions Later

Just as he is about to leave the seedy Mos Eisley cantina, intergalactic smuggler Han Solo (Harrison Ford) finds himself staring into the barrel of a blaster pistol. It is held by the scaly hands of the alien bounty hunter, Greedo (Paul Blake). Han retraces his steps and sits back down in his seat. Greedo sits opposite of him and explains, in his alien language, that he will forcibly take Han to the ruthless crime lord Jabba the Hutt, dead or alive. During this explanation, Han, while still being held at gunpoint, slowly removes his own weapon from its holster. Once Greedo finishes making his threats, but just before he can make an attempt on Han's life, the smuggler shoots and kills the bounty hunter.

If you're watching the theatrical or VHS versions of *Star Wars,* that is. If you're watching the versions released on DVD and Blu-Ray, the sequence proceeds as follows: everything is the same until Greedo finishes his threats. Then, in a clearly computer-modified monstrosity of a scene, Greedo shoots at Han from point blank range, misses the broad side of a barn that is his head, and then (or at about the same time, depending on the specific version) is shot dead by Solo.

This editing job is arguably the most controversial change made to the original *Star Wars* films. George Lucas defends the "addition," saying that Greedo actually *does* shoot in the original version, but the camera angles used to depict the scene make it hard to tell that this is the case (qtd. in Block). Lucas believes that this change is necessary to clarify that Han Solo is not "a cold-blooded killer" (qtd. in Block). This idea presumes, with moderate accuracy from what I can tell, that many *Star Wars* fans who oppose the change want Han to shoot first because it establishes his morally ambiguous, "antihero" character. If these are the only two "popular" sides of this debate, then I don't fit in anywhere. I firmly believe that Han shot first, but I've never considered him anything other than a full-fledged hero. To me, both of the "popular" opinions say essentially the same thing: that shooting someone who is about to shoot you is *wrong*. What? Seriously? I would call Han's reaction a fairly natural and logical one. It doesn't *make* him a hero by any means, but this act of simple self-preservation certainly shouldn't *prevent* him from being one.

Han Solo is just one of many characters "victimized" by an assumed set of standards that say that heroes in movies can never kill, or at least can only kill under ridiculously extreme and specific circumstances. These standards not only demand a higher suspension of disbelief and a separation between film and reality, they also deny audiences the full, thought-provoking potential of movies. Ultimately, these standards fail to recognize that sometimes, a film works better when the hero kills rather than spares.

Don't get me wrong; I like it when a hero can find an effective way to apprehend the bad guys without killing them. Some movies, however, seem to "shoehorn" in some no-killing morality where it otherwise doesn't fit, just to satisfy these assumed standards, and this often forces the audience to suspend more disbelief than they should have to. Christopher Nolan's *Dark Knight* Trilogy, where Batman's (Christian Bale) only rule is that he won't kill, is a good example. I really, *really* love these films, and the "one rule" of no killing is an important part of Batman's character, so this morality does fit from an adaptation standpoint, but in relation to the events of the films, it fits much less. The filmmakers go above and beyond in emphasizing the rule and how it gives Batman a huge moral high ground over his foes. That sounds great, but I think that the audience really needs to ask an important question: *does* it give him that much of a high ground? Is breaking several bones in someone's body and leaving them without medical attention really that much better than killing them? A little bit, maybe, but depending on how serious the maiming is, the recipient of such a beating might *wish* they were dead, and *I* would almost prefer it if Batman would oblige them. Also, as Tom Baker points out in his article, "10 Movie Heroes Who Killed More Than The Villains," the one rule is proven ineffective in *The Dark Knight Rises,* where Selina Kyle (Anne Hathaway) has to *kill* Bane (Tom Hardy)—using the weapons mounted on the motorcycle belonging to the supposedly non-lethal Batman, I might add—in order to save Batman's life. The Dark Knight isn't even good at *following* his questionable rule, much less justifying it. Throughout the trilogy, Batman is at least indirectly responsible for a handful of deaths, such as leaving Ra's Al Ghul (Liam Neeson) to die in *Batman Begins* and causing Harvey Dent (Aaron Eckhart) to fall off of a building in *The Dark Knight* (Baker). I can count several more instances where the property damage Batman causes (during a literally explosive car chase in *The Dark Knight,* for example) would have realistically led to even more fatalities, of criminals and innocents alike.

I don't let these discrepancies get in the way of my viewing pleasure, but upon reflection, they do hurt the film's logic. Batman *says* he doesn't kill, but if the audience is to take him at his word, they have to ignore the details of many on-screen and implied events. Batman clearly doesn't follow his rule perfectly, and maybe the point of the films is that it's impossible for him to do so. That would be an interesting angle, but Batman's following of the rule is rarely, if ever, questioned in the movies, so I don't think that was the point.

Then why stress the no killing rule so much, or have it at all? Outside of character adaptation, my theory is that, when writing *Batman Begins,* the filmmakers originally made a movie that downplayed or perhaps didn't even include the one rule at all, but later squeezed it in and packed a ton of emphasis on it in order to meet the strict moral standards that they assumed their audience would have. But really, the one rule *causes* a bigger moral dilemma than it solves. If Batman just killed some criminals and caused some collateral damage in the process (as he does in the movies), without trying to explain it away, he would be forced to contend with accusations (from other characters and from audiences) of being a dangerous vigilante who plays judge, jury, and executioner. Since he *does* try to explain it away, however, Batman could still be called all of those things, as well as a self-deceiving *liar.* What was that stuff about gaining moral high ground? If the intention behind adhering to these standards was to make Batman seem more heroic, it might have actually accomplished the *opposite* effect.

If you still don't see what I mean when I say that these standards necessitate a higher suspension of disbelief, just watch the edited version of *Star Wars.* The cantina scene is so sloppy and so stupid that it is no longer anywhere close to believable, even for a space fantasy movie. George Lucas was so committed to meeting strict standards about killing that he sacrificed the quality of the film, and this should never be the case. I would much rather watch a believable movie with a hero that kills than a cartoonish joke with a non-lethal hero (unless the movie is *supposed* to be a cartoon or a joke, in which case I can excuse much more silliness).

The assumed standards do more than just threaten the believability of films; they can demand a complete separation between the reality of a movie and the reality of, well, *reality.* Baker's assessment of *Where Eagles Dare* protagonist Lieutenant Schaffer (Clint Eastwood) illustrates this double standard. He begins his entry on it as follows:

> Okay, so we suppose that technically the villains of *Where Eagles Dare* are the Nazis, in which case the bad guys have a pretty depressingly huge body count. That's entirely too morbid for us, however, so let's just take a look at how many people cark it over the course of this 1968 action classic.

I may have agreed with some of what Baker noticed about Batman, but I can't say the same here. Baker claims that, when considering only the deaths within the movie, the heroes kill more than the villains, and he seems to imply that this fact makes Lieutenant Schaffer and his allies less "heroic." This might be the case when the film is analyzed in such a way, but really, Baker has no right to judge the movie as separate from history. World War II is not just the inspiration for the film, it's the *setting,* and therefore the actual circumstances of the war must be taken into account, regardless of how "morbid" they may be. The audience is supposed to derive sympathy for Lieutenant Schaffer at least partially from the fact that he is fighting a murderous, tyrannical regime that once conquered nearly all of Europe and sought to completely eradicate certain peoples from existence. Without being tied to real-life history, the movie can't possibly work, and it shouldn't be expected to do so.

This separation with reality is where I believe George Lucas got his rationale for modifying the Cantina scene. He judged Han Solo by standards so strict that it was deemed unacceptable to kill someone holding him at gunpoint unless the lead (or energy bolts, as it were) started flying from the "bad guy's" end first. Movie heroes are often held to these ridiculous standards, but are people in real life held to them? I know I wouldn't hold anyone to them. If someone is about to be killed by someone else in real life, they should do whatever they can to stay alive. Lucas may hold people in real life to oddly strict standards when it comes to killing, in which case, while I disagree, he is in the right in holding movie characters to them as well. But if he's *only* holding movie characters to these standards, this is a very, *very* bad situation. In order to make a space fantasy film like *Star Wars,* you need to bend quite a few rules of reality, but there still needs to be *some* sort of common ground in order for the audience to connect with the movie, and morality should never be one of those bent rules (unless the point of the film is to satirize or criticize certain aspects of commonly-held morality, but you would have to work really hard to convince me that this is supposed to be going on in *Star Wars*). When films are expected to be *completely* insulated from the rules of real life, they face unwarranted judgment that makes them out to be worse movies than they actually are. These movies are faced with two equally disastrous options when under this scrutiny: they can either endure the undue bad press indefinitely (like how *Where Eagles Dare* endures Baker's criticism), or they can get artificially modified to meet the assumed standards, resulting in damaged logic (which may have been the case in the *Dark Knight* trilogy) or even more backlash and controversy (as was the case with *Star Wars*).

I reject these expectations that urge films and their heroes to be unnecessarily unbelievable and unrealistic. Why? Well, to answer that, I turn not to an argument for more realistic *heroes,* but to an argument for more realistic *villains.* In his researched argument, "Villains in Film: Anemic Renderings," Stuart Fischoff provides reasons to invest in better movie villains, and these well-stated reasons directly parallel the reasons *I* would give for needing better *heroes.*

Complexity is the first key to better characters. Fischoff states, "Fact: True-life villains in situ do not giggle and chortle unless they are simultaneously inhaling nitrous oxide" (708). A similar observation can be made of heroes: real heroes don't stand with their fists poised on their waist with a cape and a flag waving behind them. Real heroism and villainy are much more complex, as Fischoff elaborates using the specific example of *The Godfather:* "what's most fascinating about Francis Ford Coppola's *Godfather* trilogy and the Mafia legend is that the Mafiosi are shown doing such villainous deeds, yet at the same time, they are shown as capable of being loving parents and grandparents, committed to certain values" (710). Just as the best villains are shown as not being "all bad," the best heroes are the ones who aren't "spotless." They need to have personal demons and they need to be seen performing actions that aren't always "heroic"—this is where killing can come in. Good heroes need to contend with the past, with their emotions, and with their *methods,* and the most poignant heroes are the ones that the audience can *see* deal with such problems, rather than having them already sorted out by the first frame. These issues don't make these characters into antiheroes, they just make them more realistic and more relatable to the audience, and the most relatable hero is the most impactful, if not the most heroic.

Speaking of relatability, connection with the audience is the second key to better characters. Fischoff claims, "To understand others' villainy ... we need only look into ourselves at our weakest, most enraged, or most desperate and vengeful moments" (708). In the same vein, we should be able to understand heroes in movies by analyzing our strongest, most selfless, and most courageous moments, not by appealing to a sense of "unobtainable goodness." Film heroes need to have enough imperfections for the audience to believe that such a character could exist in real life, and loosening the rules around killing may be necessary in order to accomplish this. Fischoff adds, "We console ourselves with the thought that villains are twisted aliens. Consequently, what makes a villain truly interesting is to glimpse his or her nonalien, distinctly human rationalization of these values" (709). Just as we hide from our flaws through superficially evil villains, we sell our virtues short when we expect film heroes to be something unrealistically good. Heroes need to be vessels through which audiences can realize the good that is naturally in them, and automatically excluding from the "hero club" everyone who kills or has killed under any circumstance other than the most ridiculously extreme doesn't exactly help in this respect—for example, if we were to apply this sort of morality to real life, all soldiers would be (quite wrongfully, in my opinion) denied the title of hero.

Good film heroes, by ultimately doing the right thing despite their flaws (and perhaps despite a dead villain), should inspire other characters, and especially the audience, to become the heroes that *they* were born to be.

Even more important than inspiring heroism, film heroes should inspire *critical thought,* and at times this can be connected to the act of killing. This is certainly the case in *Dirty Harry,* where inspector Harry Callahan's (Clint Eastwood, again) lethal decision provides some interesting food for thought for the audience. In the film, Callahan pursues a mass murderer, Scorpio (Andy Robinson), who extorts the government to pay him in order to stop the killings. Callahan gets close to bringing Scorpio to justice multiple times, but "bureaucratic authority" (Lichtenfeld 20) always gets in the way, saying that the killer must be released because Harry violated his Constitutional rights. Scorpio continues to kill innocent people after he is released, until Callahan bucks the chain of command by going after him one last time. After an intense chase, the two are armed and face-to-face. Callahan offers to accept a surrender from Scorpio in the form of a memorable "Are you feeling lucky?" monologue, but the murderer refuses. Just as the criminal raises his weapon to shoot Callahan, the inspector shoots Scorpio (sounds an awful lot like the cantina scene in *Star Wars,* doesn't it?) and then, as interpreted by film critic Pauline Kael, "Harry throws his [badge] into the water (the same water into which his Magnum has just blown Scorpio's body), out of contempt for the law itself" (qtd. in 20).

As much as *I* think that this chain of events invites thought, some others simply brush it off. Eric Lichtenfeld, in his book *Action Speaks Louder,* believes that Harry Callahan's contention with the law merely displays "the conservative politics" of the film as well as "a counterintuitive strain of libertarianism" (20). He cites author Eric Patterson, who claims that the anti-authoritarian messages in the film are "repressive rather than progressive," since they direct these powerful feelings that audiences already have in ways "which will not lead to disruption of existing structures" (qtd. in 20).

I wouldn't so quickly say that Harry's actions are cinematically useless. Sure, maybe *Dirty Harry* hasn't inspired anyone to write a petition or join a protest, and thank God it hasn't (to my knowledge) inspired uncontrolled vigilantism. Perhaps the movie hasn't directly contributed to institutional change, but I don't think that the filmmakers intended for that to be the effect—they intended to get people *thinking.* On the surface, they may appeal to themes of rebellion against authority in order to boost ticket sales, but the movie itself goes deeper than that. *Dirty Harry* seriously challenges the morality of a legal system that seems to value the rights of a serial killer above the rights of his victims and their families. The filmmakers wanted the viewers to consider that, if the law were to indeed become so warped, then maybe, in the words of Dirty Harry himself, "the law's crazy!" (qtd. in Lichtenfeld 19–20).

Watching a movie is hardly sufficient reason to take vigilante action, but it's plenty reason to adopt vigilante *thought*. As much as we hate to think about it, governments can go seriously wrong anywhere—Germany, circa 1933, was considered by the rest of the world to be one of the most civilized societies that ever existed—and the only way we can prevent this from happening to us is to analyze our government with great scrutiny and distrust and decide whether or not the law has become "crazy." This cuts both ways; we need to use just as much scrutiny when we think the government is doing too little (like in *Dirty Harry*) as we do when we think that it may be doing too much (such as TSA security procedures and the recent nationwide allegations of police brutality).

Dirty Harry, in effect, asks audience members to be rational, conscientious individuals. As stated by Enlightenment philosopher Immanuel Kant in *Grounding for the Metaphysics of Morals,* "Everything in nature works according to laws. Only a rational being has the power to act according to his *conception* [italics added] of the laws, i.e., according to *principles,* and thereby has he a will" (23). Harry fits Kant's idea of a rational being; by killing Scorpio, Callahan not only practices basic self-defense, he rejects blind adherence to the law in exchange for a more stable morality based on his *conception* of the law through the lens of *principle*. The movie uses Harry's outwardly-visible situation in order to illustrate the internal process that the audience is intended to experience; Harry challenges moviegoers to consider that perhaps "right" and "wrong" should be the highest principles, rather than "legal" and "illegal," and regardless of whether or not the conclusion is correct, this call to critical thinking is the most heroic action of them all.

When a hero in a movie kills his or her adversary, it can mean quite a bit more than you might think. Whether right or wrong, killing is sometimes necessary in order to preserve the believability and realism of a film and in order to inspire the audience to think critically. Therefore, audiences should put just as much critical thought into the acceptability of each individual lethal action, instead of just unilaterally deeming them all to be wrong.

When such critical thought is used, I see that Han Solo "shooting first" accomplishes all three of the major positive effects of a lethal action. Han firing the first shot looks much more believable than the alternative—after all, would a seasoned bounty hunter really miss a shot at point-blank range? If I were in Han's shoes, I would have shot first as well, so to me, this action ties the film more securely to reality. Finally, Solo's killing hand has inspired me to wrap my head around some philosophical thought (as if this paper wasn't already evidence of that): if he *hadn't* killed Greedo, he would likely be dead or imprisoned, in which case Princess Leia (Carrie Fischer) would have never been rescued, the Death Star would have never been destroyed, and the Rebellion may very well have been crushed by the Galactic Empire. Is it possible that a "good" act (such as not killing) can be overshadowed by all of the bad consequences that come as a result? In the end, we, as audiences, should be *thanking* Han Solo and all other film heroes who have killed; they shot first, and in so doing, they gave us something to ask questions about later.

Works Cited

Baker, Tom. "10 Movie Heroes Who Killed More Than The Villains." *What Culture*. n. p. 21 Sept. 2014. Web. 27 Oct. 2015. http://whatculture.com/film/10-movie-heroes-killed villains.php.

Batman Begins. Dir. Christopher Nolan. Perf. Christian Bale, Liam Neeson, and Michael Caine. Warner Brothers, 2005. Film

Block, Alex Ben. "5 Questions With George Lucas: Controversial 'Star Wars' Changes, SOPA and 'Indiana Jones 5.'" *The Hollywood Reporter*. The Hollywood Reporter, 9 Feb. 2012. Web. 3 Nov. 2015. http://www.hollywoodreporter.com/heat-vision/george-lucas star-wars-interview-288523

The Dark Knight. Dir. Christopher Nolan. Perf. Christian Bale, Heath Ledger, and Aaron Eckhart. Warner Brothers, 2008. Film.

The Dark Knight Rises. Dir. Christopher Nolan. Perf. Christian Bale, Tom Hardy, and Anne Hathaway. Warner Brothers, 2012. Film.

Dirty Harry. Dir. Don Siegel. Perf. Clint Eastwood, Andy Robinson, and Harry Guardino. Warner Brothers, 1971. DVD.

Fischoff, Stuart. "Villains in Film: Anemic Renderings." *Bedford Book of Genres: A Guide and Reader*. Ed. Amy Braziller and Elizabeth Kleinfeld. Boston: Bedford/St. Martin's, 2014. 706–713. Print.

Kant, Immanuel. *Grounding for the Metaphysics of Morals with On a Supposed Right to Lie Because of Philanthropic Concerns*. Trans. James W. Ellington. Indianapolis: Hackett Publishing, 1993. 23. Print.

Lichtenfeld, Eric. *Action Speaks Louder: Violence, Spectacle, and the American Action Movie*. Connecticut: Praeger Publishers, 2004. 19–20. Print.

Star Wars. Dir. George Lucas. Perf. Mark Hamill, Harrison Ford, and Carrie Fischer. 20th Century Fox, 1977. DVD and VHS.

Where Eagles Dare. Dir. Brian G. Hutton. Perf. Richard Burton, Clint Eastwood, and Mary Ure. Mero-Goldwyn-Mayer, 1968. DVD.

Questions to Consider

1. David begins his essay by telling the story of a particular scene in *Star Wars* and holds off giving readers the main idea of his essay until after the first few paragraphs. What did you think about this technique? In what contexts might it be more effective to have a longer introduction before telling the reader the main idea of the essay?
2. Although many students are told that they should always write academic papers in third person, in David's essay, he writes in first person and uses "I" at various places throughout. Where does he use "I" and when does he write in third person? What possible effects might there be upon readers in making this choice? In what contexts is it appropriate to write in first person? How about third person? Does it change how you interpret the writer? How?
3. David uses a variety of examples to illustrate his point in this essay. Why might he have chosen these particular examples? Were you able to relate to some or all of them? Can you think of other examples that either support or refute his claim? How effective did you find the examples that he chose to use?

Stress: Not Just a Matter of Time

Stephen Bothwell
Second Runner Up Winner | Research-Based Argument

Reflection

As a college student, stress is just something that I, among many others, have to deal with. However, I really wanted to become more informed about stress so that I could tackle it better. In a previously taken psychology course, I had discovered that one's perspective on stress is key to how the body deals with stress. Wanting to gain a better grip on this perspective and on what exactly the problems of stress often are, I used this paper concerning causal arguments as a stepping stone for my own betterment; after all, knowing the root of the problem of stress for college students would assuredly help me as a college student.

After using Xavier's resources for research on the topic of stress and its prevalence in the lives of college students, I wanted to start by putting my own creative spin on the paper. We had previously discussed the appeals of pathos, logos, and ethos with our professor in the course and I felt that I had largely stuck to using logos and ethos to drive my points thus far. I could not see how exactly to figure pathos into the paper without damaging my argument. Surely, it seemed like an emotional argument would decrease my ethos in that I might seem too passionate about the issue and, therefore, irrationally passionate about one point of view. I decided to write a narrative-based emotional argument so that I could relate an experience to a wider audience and have a more effective appeal overall. Originally, I related stress to a flame that burned a person from within. Yet, after peer reviews and a meeting with my professor, this metaphor did not seem to mesh well with the rest of my argument. The passionate and abstract nature of the metaphor was too much, so I changed the metaphor from flame to time and made its tone and concreteness gel more coherently with the rest of the piece. I was really glad that I was able to use this type of appeal that seldom appears in my formal works. It is really important, in my opinion, to make sure that a writer does not forget that they, too, have an argumentative voice.

Stress: Not Just a Matter of Time

The clock is ticking; time is running out. The dreaded *tick* and *tock* of some timepiece echoes through the air as college students scribble away on tests, trying desperately to finish. Time does no favors; those who look at the clock are reminded of what little time remains. With so much left to do and so few minutes remaining, panic sets in. Pessimism and hopelessness worm their way into students' minds, causing them to regret that they did not study longer.

As the test concludes, many worry about their work and end up viewing the rest of their day in the same worrisome, negative light. Indeed, many, including myself, have been in this situation; tests, papers, presentations, jobs, family matters, and many other daily obligations can cause this horrid sensation. Unfortunately, this feeling is the reality of stress—in more distinct terms, a feeling of discomfort in response to current circumstances that provokes a biological response—for many college students, and it is not one that is receding (Baum, qtd. in Alvord et al.).

An increasing amount of stress for college students is clearly evidenced by statistics. The American Psychological Association (APA) has reported with data from the Center for Collegiate Mental Health that the number of students that visit counseling services has gone up from 45.2% to 48.7% between 2010 and 2013 (Novotney 36). The Association for University and College Counseling Center Directors further reports that the main factor of this increase is student anxiety, increasing from about 37% to 46% in students seeking help from 2007 to 2013 (Novotney 36). It becomes clear that this severe uptick in anxiety—that is, "a reaction to something that may happen in the future" which usually occurs in response to stress—is a problem for many college students that must be examined (Mishkova). I posit that students have become increasingly obligated to do more in college and, because of this, get less of the meaningful interaction that they need to relieve stress. Furthermore, because student counseling resources are overwhelmed with requests, students are not able to work through their stresses properly and perpetuate their stress in a grim cycle through a negative perspective on stress.

The cycle of student stress begins with the college environment and, specifically, the amount of obligations that students have in dealing with all of the changes that come with college life. A clear depiction of all of the challenges that an average student must face appears in an article by Florida International University that utilizes survey results from its own Counseling and Psychological Services as evidence. The writer, a college student herself, reports that, for college students, approximately 56 hours a week are dedicated to sleep, followed by 48 hours to studying, 35 hours to work, 12 hours to class, and 10 hours to commuting (Graham). This leaves 19 hours to, as the author states, "socialize, maintain a healthy lifestyle and attend to family obligations," which are all grouped under "free time" in the writer's data (Graham). Yet, these 19 hours are not stress-free as the term "free time" might imply, as they must be spent eating and caring for oneself on each of the seven days of the week. With the bulk of their time spent upon various tasks and obligations imposed by their college life, students really do not get much time for themselves to think, to relax, and to socialize meaningfully with others. Since college students have a greater number of obligations, they have less time to recognize and to respond to their stresses properly, allowing for their stresses to build up.

Because many college students do not recognize that the body's stress response promotes social interaction, they cannot take advantage of the response and deal with their stress naturally. Kelly McGonigal, a health psychologist, reports that when oxytocin, a brain chemical, is released during stress, "it is motivating you to seek support … instead of bottling [the stress] up." In other words, the body naturally produces a chemical that encourages social interaction to work through stress. This understanding is also supported by a study performed by Windsor University psychologists that examined the relation between academic stress and loneliness. The study found "academic coping to be a mediating factor for academic stressors, in particular, in the relation between loneliness and academic performance" (Stoliker and Lafreniere 158). This notion of academic coping can exist in three forms: as approaching the problem alone, as avoiding the problem, or as seeking social support for the problem (Stoliker and Lafreniere 151). Their study showed that academic coping was effective in dealing with academic stressors, especially with loneliness. Specifically, most students chose the approach option and went at their stress alone (Stoliker and Lafreniere 154). Many do not consider that interaction with others might alleviate their stress. In fact, only .27% of students thought that loneliness was their problem (Stoliker and Lafreniere 156). Of course, many of the students here likely recognize that there are ways to tackle stress alone. Yet, very few students realize that social interaction is a natural mediator of stress and, because of this, are probably still facing stress. As there are times when college students do need others to help them work through stress, not knowing that they need others to work with to overcome their stresses can be a big obstacle.

As for the students who do feel a need to work with others to overcome their stresses, they often face another problem: a lack of counselor staffing and long waiting lists that do not permit those who need assistance to get it. As the APA reports, "One of the biggest reasons why college and university counseling services are seeing an increase in the number of people requesting help and in the severity of their cases is simply that more people are now attending college" (Novotney 36). Yet, while an increased college population would logically lead to an increased number of counselor visits, this is not the whole story. While the amount of college students has increased, "many center budgets remain unchanged or have increased only slightly from years past," thereby not accommodating to students' need for help with their stress-related issues (Novotney 36). Some universities are not adapting financially to the demands of an increased population of those who need mental help, but even those who are doing so have trouble. For example, when the University of Florida hired three more counselors, the university only had "two weeks without a waiting list" and did not have the lasting solution that it thought it did (Novotney 36).

This example makes it clear that new ways of giving students the necessary help and counselor interaction must be explored, as increasing the number of counselors only slows the waiting list. If universities cannot bolster their counseling services so that those who realize that they need psychological help can receive it, students will not get the interaction that they need to relieve loneliness and to surmount their stresses, causing their stress to persist.

If students cannot stop their stress from persisting, their perspective on stress will likely perpetuate the cycle of stress that they experience. As the University of Florida's Counseling and Wellness Center astutely states, "Before condemning stress outright, we need to understand that stress is only harmful when it is excessive" ("Stress and College Students"). However, it is more likely that most see stress as harmful in most, if not all, situations. Kelly McGonigal notes this view through her own experience: "My confession is this: I am a health psychologist, and my mission is to help people be happier and healthier. But I fear that something I've been teaching for the last 10 years is doing more harm than good ... Basically, I've turned stress into the enemy." If this is the perspective of a health psychologist, someone who has been a part of the psychological field for a decent period of time, what are students likely to think? It is plain to see that they would unknowingly consider it to be negative, as it often occurs during challenging or difficult situations. If students continue to think that stress is a detrimental feeling, they will only continue to feel negatively about it, leading to more stress involving whatever it is about the college environment that is already stressful and perpetuating the cycle of stress.

College students have seen an increase in stress because of a stressful cycle that has formed for them. These students have a large amount of obligations and duties that they must fulfill, leading to less time for social interaction. Because they do not have a regular amount of time for social interaction and often do not understand interaction's role in the stress response, college students cannot relieve stress properly. As for those that do see that they need help with their stress, especially when it is more serious, they usually cannot visit counselors because of long waiting lists that are not remedied by simply hiring more employees. When all of this stress is bottled up and is viewed as something wholly negative, rather than as something that is only negative when it is excessive, the stress that students have can easily be exacerbated and augmented. As a student myself, I have always seen stress as a real issue. Stress is not just a matter of time—for many, stress does not just fade away as minutes stretch into hours and hours into days. For the sake of all current and future college students, we must innovate new solutions to the grim cycle of stress so that stress, instead of working against us, might just work for us.

Works Cited

Alvord, Mary K., et al. "Understanding Chronic Stress." *American Psychological Association.* American Psychological Association, n.d. Web. 4 Apr. 2016.

Baum, A. "Stress, Intrusive Imagery, and Chronic Distress." *Health Psychology* 9.6 (1990): 653–675. Web. 4 Apr. 2016.

Graham, Amanda. "Surveys Show Increase in Stress Among College Students." *FIU News.* Florida International University, 2015. Web. 28 Mar. 2016.

McGonigal, Kelly. "How to Make Stress Your Friend." Online video clip. *TED.* TED, 2013. Web. 28 Mar. 2016.

Mishkova, Gergana. "Stress versus Anxiety." *Sutter Health: Palo Alto Medical Foundation.* Palo Alto Medical Foundation, July 2013. Web. 4 Apr. 2016.

Novotney, Amy. "Students Under Pressure." *Monitor on Psychology 45*.8 (2014): 36. Web. 28 Mar. 2016.

Stoliker, Bryce E., and Kathryn D. Lafreniere. "The Influence of Perceived Stress, Loneliness, and Learning Burnout on University Students' Educational Experience." *College Student Journal 49*.1 (2015): 146–160. Web. 4 Apr. 2016.

"Stress and College Students." *UF: Counseling & Wellness Center.* University of Florida, n.d. Web. 28 Mar. 2016.

Questions to Consider

1. At the beginning of this essay, Stephen uses vivid description to illustrate how stress feels for students in college. How relatable did you find this description? How does it contrast in tone with the rest of his essay? Did you think this was an effective way of bringing readers into his argument and connecting it to their daily lives? What other strategies might he have employed?
2. In this essay, Stephen posits causality for the problem of stress. How does he arrange his argument to support his claims? What kind of reasoning does he use? What information comes first, second, third, etc.? Is this an effective arrangement for this argument? Why or why not?
3. Stephen uses a variety of sources in his paper and does not rely upon a strategy that leads to a "one source per paragraph" arrangement. How does he use sources in his argument to support his claims? Does this make his argument more effective? How would his paper have been different if he had focused solely on one source per paragraph?

D'Artagnan Award Honorable Mention

Category: Rhetorical Analysis

The next genre of writing we will explore is the Rhetorical Analysis, a type of analytic approach for interpreting texts, which focuses on rhetorical appeals that work to persuade an audience. As discussed in the "Rhetorical Terms and Appeals" section near the beginning of this book, rhetoric examines particular aspects of persuasive texts in order to understand how they work. In a rhetorical analysis, you will be asked to analyze texts—which could be magazine ads, editorials, political speeches, images, videos, newspaper articles, commercials, or a host of other types of texts—from a rhetorical perspective.

While students often have background with analysis prior to coming to college, many first year writers report that the rhetorical analysis is a new genre for them. Because of that, examples of this type of essay may be helpful to you so that you can get an idea of what might be expected in an analysis of this sort. Although your instructor may have specific guidelines and type of assignment that are different from the examples you see here, all rhetorical analyses ask the writer to investigate a text to see how it operates rhetorically. You might consider aspects of a text such as pathos (how the text moves the emotions of the audience), ethos (the authority or character of the speaker/writer), and logos (how logically an argument is presented), as well as the timing of the text you are critiquing, the context in which it was published or distributed, the audience for which it was intended, the style or tone it takes in order to connect with the audience, etc. By engaging in rhetorical analysis, you will become more aware of the rhetorical texts around you in your everyday life and be able to discern the ways in which you are persuaded. Additionally, through this awareness, you can learn to craft more rhetorically effective texts yourself, as you will when you create various arguments as part of your classroom assignments.

In our first selection, "How Cassidy Argues Snowden's Heroism," Christina Peterman examines an argument in support of Edward Snowden as a hero. In her analysis, Christina notes that the author of the article makes strong appeals to both character and logic, but may overlook the power of engaging the readers' emotions. The editorial team was impressed by the way she focused on the context of the article—when and where it was published—as well as her attention to stylistic devices, such as hypophora and rhetorical questions, which engage the audience. Her understanding of the way that this author constructs his own ethos, and the subtle shifts made throughout the article to convince the audience of Snowden's heroism, demonstrates the type of sophisticated investigation we hope to see in a rhetorical analysis essay.

Our next essay, "The Bold Eloquence of Bernie Sanders," is the second selection in this book written by Stephen Bothwell, whose research-based argument won Second Runner Up overall. His essay looks at the speech given by Sanders on May 26, 2015 wherein he announced his intention to run for president. The editorial team appreciated how Stephen highlights Sanders's use of narrative and emotion in order to connect to the audience, making it more likely that they will heed his call to action. Stephen shows how political speeches work rhetorically and offers a well-organized approach to a rhetorical analysis.

Both Christina and Stephen arranged their essays in a way that walks readers through the text they are analyzing in a logical fashion without resorting to an organizational scheme that is broken down in a simple "three points" fashion based upon pathos, ethos, and logos. While it may be easy to arrange a rhetorical analysis in a format where you analyze each of these three appeals, one per paragraph, this often leads to segregating the appeals more discretely than is optimal. Often, an argument may rely upon multiple appeals at once; for instance, a strong appeal to reason—such as statistical data or verifiable facts—may also serve to build the ethos of the writer as someone who is an expert in his or her field. While analyzing rhetorical appeals "separately" may make for an easy organizational strategy, it often leads to less sophisticated analysis.

As you read these essays, note the way that Christina and Stephen highlight aspects of the texts they are analyzing, showing how these texts work to persuade, engage, and move a reader to hold a particular point of view or take a certain action. When you begin to analyze texts rhetorically, you will become more aware of how you are persuaded, as well as how you use rhetorical appeals in your own everyday life.

How Cassidy Argues Snowden's Heroism

Christina Peterman
Rhetorical Analysis

Reflection

I knew as soon as I began the writing process for this Rhetorical Analysis that I wanted to examine an article centering on the issue of Edward Snowden. The whole class was focused on issues of free speech, and of all the issues we examined throughout the semester that was the one that most fascinated me. My only hesitation going in was that I had already formed an opinion on the question of Snowden's guilt, and therefore I struggled in deciding whether I wanted to analyze an article that I agreed or disagreed with. In the end I decided on one I agreed with, and therefore chose Cassidy's article. Therefore, my biggest challenge throughout the writing process was to keep my opinion out of my writing and remain clinical and detached in my analysis.

After in-class peer review I revised a lot of my word choices and sentence structure to make my paper appear less biased. One thing I found on every assignment throughout the semester was that it was always very surprising just how many edits I was able to make on my own paper, even after reviewing it so many times. Every time I took a paper to the writing center, my professor, or to a classmate during peer-review there was always something I ended up changing. I believe it was this process and these edits that allowed the final product to be as unbiased as it was, because no matter how hard we might try on our own, writers always bring in a certain level of personal bias. Therefore, I would advise every writer—from beginners to experts, to take advantage of the review process many more times than you might believe necessary, as others are always more apt to catch things that we ourselves might not notice. I promise your paper will be better for it in the end, as I know mine was.

How Cassidy Argues Snowden's Heroism

The question of Edward Snowden's guilt is one of the most convoluted and multifaceted issues to face modern America. Although it may not seem like its ramifications could possibly be that vast or far-reaching, the implications of our decision as a society on this could affect social change throughout the decade. Most people have self-divided into two groups: either Snowden is a hero or a criminal. John Cassidy, author of *The New Yorker* article "Why Edward Snowden is a Hero," clearly falls into the first category. He wrote this article to argue not only that Snowden should not be prosecuted, but also that he should be considered a national hero. Cassidy uses ethos, logos, and a variety of stylistic devices to effectively convince the reader of Snowden's merit, but in focusing so strongly on appeals to character and logic, he overlooks the potential power of a pathos appeal.

Before any attempt can be made as to determine the way in which Cassidy argues his point, one must understand the context in which he was writing. Cassidy is an author, writer, and staff contributor to *The New Yorker,* as well as the former editor of both *The Sunday Times of London* and the *New York Post.* He elected to publish his article in *The New Yorker,* an online and in print magazine typically considered left leaning. Published on June 10, 2013, the article came out at the peak of the Snowden catastrophe. The audience he was addressing was anyone who reads *The New Yorker,* and around this time would be anyone interested in the Snowden controversy. The readership of *The New Yorker* is typically liberal minded young adults. He chooses this audience because he believes it will be the most receptive to his message and argument regarding Snowden's guilt.

Cassidy's article centers around this question of guilt; he examines whether or not Snowden's leaking of classified government documents to the people of the United States was legal under the First Amendment. There is great controversy surrounding this issue because the government considers his actions to be illegal and equivalent to espionage under the Patriot Act and Espionage Act. In fact, in June 2013 when this article was published, Edward Snowden was considered to be hiding in Hong Kong to avoid U.S. prosecution. Therefore, one of the purposes of this article was to persuade the American public that he did not deserve to be prosecuted. Cassidy spends the duration of the article arguing why Snowden's actions were justified, necessary, and even heroic.

One of the ways Cassidy makes his argument so effective is by acknowledging the opposing viewpoints on this issue. In his first paragraph, he links to the opinion of one of his colleagues, Jeffery Toobin, whom he explicitly states disagrees with him. He also quotes James Clapper, Obama's director of National Intelligence at the time as saying that Snowden did "huge grave damage to [the United States] intelligence capabilities" (Cassidy). In this way, Cassidy creates an ethos appeal to the reader: he lets the reader know that he himself understands how complex and multifaceted this issue really is, and how differing but valid opinions exist. In this way he builds credibility with the reader, who now knows that not only has Cassidy looked at the different sides of the issue, he is able to refute those sides.

Cassidy further builds his personal ethos appeal by giving examples and providing links for further research. In his opening paragraph, Cassidy references two cases he believes to be similar to Snowden's, that of Daniel Ellsberg and Mordechai Vanunu. By referencing these individuals, he sets up the fact that he has researched the issue fully, which adds to his credibility as an author. In addition, if one had come across either of these examples previously, one might be more inclined to agree with his argument about Snowden. In the article, he links to other articles about each of the listed individuals, so even if the reader had never heard of them, he or she would be able to do further research, and come to his or her own conclusions.

As Cassidy transitions from background information and other examples to his opinions on the issue, he simultaneously transitions from using ethos appeals to using logos appeals. The article is full of facts, statistics, data, and direct quotes, which serve to back up his point. Most of the data he uses serves to bolster his point about just how far reaching the N.S.A. data collection was. He cites the fact that "In March, 2013, alone ... the N.S.A. collected ninety-seven billion pieces of information from computer networks worldwide, and three billion of those pieces came from U.S.-based networks" (Cassidy). The numbers and facts give credibility to his argument by illustrating that the points on which he bases his argument are not simply speculation, but rather proven fact. Because the middle section of his article is so full of facts and numbers, one could argue that he overuses logos, but he does balance his statistical approach with a more familiar tone.

One of the ways in which Cassidy creates this familiar tone is through the stylistic device of hypophora, which is asking questions and then immediately answering them. In one example, he asks the reader "So, what did the leaks tell us?" and proceeds to answer the question, "First, they confirmed that the U.S. government, without obtaining any court warrants, routinely collects the phone logs of ... Americans" (Cassidy). This strategy creates the sense that he is having a dialogue with the reader and also serves to impart an engaging and conversational tone. Another important thing to note is that when he has a long winded answer to one of his questions, as he does in the example above, Cassidy orders the parts of his response numerically to give the reader clarity and allow him or her to follow along more closely with the argument. This appeals to logos as it ensures that clear and logical claims are made which are easy for the reader to comprehend. Both of these strategies allow the reader to engage more fully in the article and therefore make them more likely to agree with Cassidy's final conclusions.

One of the ways in which Cassidy sustains this engagement towards the end of the article is by including rhetorical questions and providing possible answers, unlike the more concrete question and answer pairs he gave towards the beginning. This signifies a shift in the article; while in the beginning he was providing background about the issue and could definitively answer questions, towards the end he moves on to the argument part of the article. For example, he asks questions such as "Were Clapper and Alexander deliberately lying?" and "So what is Snowden's real crime?" which have no definitive answer, but serve to engage the reader's mind (Cassidy). Cassidy acknowledges through this strategy that some of these questions have no one correct and/or discernable answer, which enables the reader to give more credit to his argument and perhaps even think more deeply about it themselves.

Cassidy does not just establish a familiar tone with fancy rhetorical devices, he also uses more simple and understated techniques. One example of this is his continued use of the first person plural throughout the article, such as when he says "Let's remind ourselves," "we now have to doubt," and "world in which we live" (Cassidy). This continued usage allows the reader to feel as though they are discovering and arguing alongside Cassidy and that his opinions are truly theirs. Cassidy also uses varied sentence structure, stacks short and long sentences, and short paragraphs to give a less academic and more journalistic feel to his writing. This allows him to capture and sustain the attention of the reader, and is a very effective technique in terms of making a convincing argument.

As opposed to Cassidy's strong use of ethos and logos, one of the weaker aspects of the article is the lack of pathos, or emotional appeal. Granted, Cassidy did reference common social media sites, phone companies, etc. to enable the average person to relate to the hacks and to feel how they personally were affected, but overall the article lacked pathos connections. The article could have been made much stronger with some sort of emotional connection to the reader that engaged their attention. For example, providing personal detail on Snowden could have allowed the reader to empathize with him and therefore be more likely to agree with Cassidy that Snowden does not deserve to be incarcerated for his actions.

Cassidy might have lacked a large presence of pathos, but overall his argumentation and rhetorical style were extremely effective. He incorporated ethos and logos while balancing out the article with a variety of rhetorical devices meant to convey a familiar and engaging tone. All of these devices and techniques served to underscore the importance of his argument and allowed the reader to follow along and maintain interest in the subject matter. Cassidy not only left the reader with a good sense of the complex nature of Snowden's guilt, but he also made a valid and convincing argument that Snowden indeed should be considered a hero.

Work Cited

Cassidy, John. "Why Edward Snowden Is a Hero." *The New Yorker*. The New Yorker, 10 June 2013. Web. 15 Oct. 2015.

Questions to Consider

1. In many texts that create an argument, there are often more rhetorical appeals to analyze than could possibly be covered in a paper of this length. How do you think Christina decided upon which appeals to cover in her paper? When you do a rhetorical analysis, what aspects of a text do you think are most important to highlight for readers?
2. As mentioned in the introduction to the Rhetorical Analysis section of this book, Christina did not organize her paper in a way that focused on one appeal at a time, or a "one appeal per paragraph" strategy. How did she choose to organize her paper? Was this a logical progression that you found easy to follow? What other strategies might she have chosen to present her analysis?
3. In her reflection, Christina mentioned that she made revisions to try to make her analysis sound less biased. Do you think she was successful in making this an impartial analysis of the article? Is it possible to present a paper without any bias at all? In what situations might it be most appropriate to remain as unbiased as possible, and when it is alright to offer your opinion?

The Bold Eloquence of Bernie Sanders

Stephen Bothwell
Rhetorical Analysis

Reflection

Being the first paper that I had to write for my rhetoric course, this piece was one that I had to work hard on so that I would catch some of my writing flaws and trouble spots as soon as possible. I did enjoy the directness of Bernie Sanders' speech, regardless of my political affiliation, and considered it a good speech to analyze. However, the problem with my writing was that it was not direct. I kept bogging myself down with passive verbs and complex sentence structures that not only made my paper hard to read through but also caused my points to become less clear and coherent. This was especially true with my thesis and topic sentences, which are especially key to showing clarity, coherence, and impact within a work. I decided to go to Xavier's Writing Center to have a crack at dealing with these issues. And, indeed, the Writing Center was quite helpful in condensing my thesis and creating better topic sentences so that the paper had a more coherent argument. Reading through the entire paper out loud, I worked with my partner to detect and amend the various errors that only cropped up because of a careful examination. We aimed to utilize more active verb constructions and to flesh out what I was really trying to say throughout the paper. I am very thankful to the Writing Center for this aid and strongly recommend them as a resource for general and specific writing issues.

The Bold Eloquence of Bernie Sanders

With the 2016 presidential cycle in full swing, it is no surprise that many candidates are attempting to be at the top of their game rhetorically. Each candidate has to develop a following from the American people in order to get anywhere near the presidential nomination; parties will not simply put up a candidate that they think could not win. Like most others, Bernie Sanders started from a prominent political position in running, but that position alone would not mean much if there was no bold declaration to back it up. On May 26th, 2015, Sanders gave a speech announcing his candidacy in his own Burlington, Vermont that displays his rhetorical proficiency. He relies on an emotional relation with the audience throughout the speech, increasing this connection by discussing a variety of issues, by creating stark contrasts, by using bold word choice, and by giving evidence of his competency. He does all of this to build up to an inspiring call to action for his campaign.

Sanders begins building up a basis of relatability with the audience by discussing a wide variety of issues. After thanking family and friends for their support in his initial address, he speaks to the crowd and calls for the "millions of working families to come together ... and to make certain that our children and grandchildren are able to enjoy a quality of life that brings them health, prosperity, security, and joy" (Sanders). As most Americans care fondly about their families and their futures, most can easily relate to and support such a goal. Furthermore, Sanders discusses various issues, such as income and wealth inequality, jobs, health care, and more, throughout the speech. Finally, he includes all Americans in an encompassing statement: "Where every person, no matter their race, their religion, their disability or their sexual orientation realizes the full promise of equality that is our birthright as Americans" (Sanders). In saying all of these things, Sanders is trying to have the audience relate to him via pathos. He attempts to convince the crowd that he really cares about the future of the country, the families of America, the biggest political issues, and the unity that many want the United States to embody. Sanders does this because he wants to have the audience see his ardor for these various poignant topics and wants to have them back him for that enthusiasm.

Sanders also emphasizes the gravity and direness of the various topics that he discusses through the power of stark contrast. For example, he strongly uses logos in saying: "My fellow Americans: this country faces more serious problems today than at any time since the Great Depression" (Sanders). The audience definitely has a grasp of the destitute and historical nature of the Great Depression. Sanders does not defend his statement about American problems with any numbers, but he does not have to; through this statement, he causes the people to feel a sense of desperation about the problem-filled times they live in, heightening a need for a strong leader (i.e., Sanders himself) to avert disaster. Similarly, in discussing unemployment, Sanders states that the "real unemployment is not the 5.4 percent you read ... it is close to 11 percent if you include those workers who have given up looking for jobs or ... working part time" and even goes further by displaying the more drastic percentages of prominent demographics. By raising the number each time, Sanders emphasizes the gravity of the problem, ever increasing that sinking fear and yearning for immediate action. The contrast reveals that the people desperately need a strong leader, a quality that could easily be present in the man discussing the severity of their issues.

While contrast can be used to show a degree of severity, it can also be used to antagonize. Indeed, Sanders uses this, too, and does not hold back in his call-outs. He maligns the rich (and, by subtle extension, some Republicans) in saying that "There is something profoundly wrong when the top one-tenth of 1 percent owns almost as much wealth as the bottom 90 percent, and when 99 percent of all new income goes to the top 1 percent" (Sanders). The alarming disparity arouses ire in the audience; some might see the rich as lazy in comparison to those who work multiple jobs just to make do. Sanders is underscoring a feeling of unfairness in the audience about their tough situations. Again, he calls out the rich by contrasting "huge tax breaks" with "children [going] hungry," nurturing a feeling that the wealthy are corrupt and unjust and do not care about poor, starving children (Sanders). This stark contrast powerfully drives the audience against the rich, who are often Sanders' opponents, and paints them as an immoral bunch. Not only does this potent contrast vilify Sanders' opposition, but it also continues to have the audience relate to Sanders in his rage against these corrupt rich men.

In order to further his relatability and to sever any ties between himself and the rich, Sanders tells a personal narrative. He relates that, "[His] father came to this country from Poland without a penny in his pocket," where they lived "in a small rent-controlled apartment" (Sanders). By discussing the real difficulty of his poor lifestyle, Sanders portrays himself as a hard-worker for getting to his present position as a senator and appears more trustworthy when compared to the unjust upper class. He also relates to many of the common people whose current reality is similar to Sanders' former one. He even brings the people hope when he declares: "I have seen the promise of America in my own life. My parents would have never dreamed that their son would be a U.S. Senator, let alone run for president" (Sanders). By displaying himself as an assiduous man who came up from very little, Sanders becomes a beacon of hope for the people, conveying that they, too, can overcome rough situations. Together, these quotes both inspire the people and drive them against the corrupt rich. In addition, Sanders completely separates himself from the wealthy through his diligence as a venerable political leader.

However, Sanders might not have driven people so powerfully toward himself and against the rich if he did not utilize such bold word choice. Very early in his speech, for example, he rallies the people toward a "revolution" in multiple aspects, which he proceeds to list off (Sanders). Surely, this bold word does not imply a feeble tweaking of societal policies, but calls for radical change. Furthermore, a "revolution" is needed, due to the "planetary crisis" and "devastating problems" of climate change, due to the campaigns filled with "political gossip, ... reckless personal attacks [and] character assassination," and due to the "grotesque level of inequality" in wealth (Sanders). In calling out all of these problems with such pathos-ridden language, there is little doubt that the people would be moved and distressed by such problematic issues. Regardless of whether or not the degree of the severity of the actual issues matches the strength of his words, these phrases do their job in showing what the people need to fight back against through their potent emotional propulsions.

After presenting what he fights for and against, Sanders advances to his main objective: to convince people to join his political campaign. In addressing an audience of those who have already elected him as the mayor of Burlington and as a United States Senator of Vermont, Bernie Sanders already has a grip in the minds of the audience as a sensible politician. However, this grip does not mean much if he cannot prove himself worthy of presidential candidacy. Near the end of his speech, he cites an occurrence of when he had already fought for the people as evidence of his competency. He reminds the audience of how he had made a stand for them in changing a useless rail yard into a beautiful, public lake shore; he says: "As mayor, I worked with the people ... We took the fight to the courts, to the legislature and to the people. And we won" (Sanders). Finally, in his call to action, he exhorts: "I ask you to join me in this campaign to build a future that works for all of us, and not just the few on top ... I welcome you aboard" (Sanders). In this statement, Sanders overtly reaches out to the entire audience to get them to join him in a moment of inspiration. Sanders banks on his establishment of his presidential competency to persuade the crowd that, with him leading the way, they will bring great change to America.

Throughout this speech, Sanders exhibits a solid capability in using rhetorical techniques. Sanders relates to most, if not all, of his audience by covering a large variety of issues. He rallies his supporters against the rich and against staggering problems by using bold word choice and stark contrast. Through telling the audience about his personal narrative, Sanders separates himself from the "corrupt" wealthy and forms an even stronger emotional connection between himself and those who have gone through a similar situation. Finally, after showing his competency in the political sphere by reminding the audience of a previous success, Sanders gives a resolute call to action to the audience with the hope of inspiring them to join his side in the presidential race. Through the potency of relatability in this speech, Sanders grapples the hearts and minds of the people to his side and against his opponents, relying upon the peoples' passion for poignant issues and their hatred of injustice to rally them to his side in the fierce political arena.

Works Cited

Sanders, Bernie. "Remarks Announcing Candidacy for President in Burlington, Vermont." *The American Presidency Project*. The American Presidency Project, 26 May 2015. Web. 3 Feb. 2016.

Questions to Consider

1. Stephen mentions in his reflection that he revised his thesis and topic sentences to make the wording of his essay more direct and easier to follow. How do these sentences work in his paper? If you go back and read them, can you note how they point the reader to the next idea and transition between topics? Did you find these sentences clear and easy to follow? Are there any changes you might have suggested if you had done peer review with Stephen?
2. Stephen also does not use an organizational strategy that relies upon a "one appeal per paragraph" method. How does he arrange his paper? Did you find this effective? Can you think of other strategies he might have used to present this information?
3. What can you learn about a text by reading a rhetorical analysis of it? What elements are similar in the essays by Christina and Stephen? What elements are different? From these examples, what do you think is the purpose of a rhetorical analysis? What should readers take away from the experience of reading one? Lastly, how might you apply this information to your own analysis or approach to reading persuasive texts?

Category: Narrative

You may be assigned a narrative in your ENGL 101 or 115 courses, though it may be called by different names. Some genres that incorporate this form of writing include personal narratives, narrative arguments, and ethnographies. In all cases, a narrative will tell a story and typically ask you to write in first person, addressing your audience as "I." Unlike more formal academic writing, narratives use vivid description and words that evoke emotion in readers, painting a picture of a situation or feeling so that your readers have the sense of "being there" when you tell your story.

Narratives can serve a variety of purposes in ENGL 101 and 115 and assignments involving narrative may vary greatly from class to class. *Personal narratives* may require you to tell a story of some aspect of your life, placing yourself within a certain cultural context, or ask you to examine an important event in your life that has shaped who you are today. An *ethnography,* which is typically an examination of a people and their cultures, may be written about yourself as a type of narrative. In this case, an assignment might require you to take a step back from your everyday assumptions and question your own cultural practices, applying an analytic lens to your own life the way an anthropologist would examine a less familiar society. A *narrative argument* uses story to make an argument where the narrative serves as a representative anecdote to illustrate a larger issue. While each of these types of assignments serves a different purpose, in all cases you would use story, description, dialog, and a first-person perspective in your writing.

In the first essay, Katie Kennedy illustrates an important event in her life through a personal narrative entitled "Hard Work Beats Talent When Talent Doesn't Work Hard." The editorial team noted Katie's adept use of dialog to illustrate to readers the words and intentions of Coach Marcy, an influential person in Katie's life. In addition to the colorful description of the grueling but rewarding softball practices she endured, Katie also skillfully connected these past experiences to the present, showing how the advice of her former coach sticks with her even today. This narrative is a solid example of how to write an engaging story that holds the attention of readers, while also offering a "pay off" of advice at the end that readers can apply to their own lives.

Jessica Stoll uses narrative as a means of both telling a story and making an argument in her piece, "A Night in Africa." Responding to a prompt to use a narrative to make an argument about speaking up in a risky situation, Jessica tells the story of visiting the Maasai in Africa and being called upon to disclose her religious experiences to them in a group setting. The editorial team enjoyed how Jessica used dialog in her story and connected this event to make a point about why it is important to communicate your perspective, even when doing so is scary or uncomfortable. This example of a narrative argument shows how this genre relies upon story to make or imply claims, which may then be stated more directly. By offering readers vivid details about her own experience, Jessica shows that she understands the hesitation others may feel in similar situations, but offers a compelling argument for why we should share our viewpoint anyway.

In your ENGL 101 or 115 classes, you may have the opportunity to write a narrative of some kind, and while your particular assignment may differ from these examples, there are guidelines of storytelling you can take away from the essays written by Katie and Jessica. As you read, notice how they tell their stories—what details they give, how you react or feel when you read, and the effects of their descriptions—and then remember these concepts when you craft your own narratives. We all tell stories in our lives every day, whether as an official assignment or not. Storytelling is an important aspect of culture and social interaction, and learning to craft an effective narrative in your writing gives you the opportunity to tell your story to wider audiences.

Hard Work Beats Talent When Talent Doesn't Work Hard

Katie Kennedy
Personal Narrative

Reflection

The task for this assignment was to write a personal narrative about an event that was important to us in 5 to 6 pages. I thought it would be difficult to find an event that I could talk about at such a great length, so I initially struggled with picking a topic. After talking about my concerns with my professor, Dr. Russell, I got a better sense of the freedoms I could take with my event and I decided I would have the most material if I used moments throughout a transformation process rather than a single moment. Talking about my experience at GenuWIN Sports Training was certainly meaningful to me because it molded me into the person I am today and it inspired me to take on challenges I would never have dared to attempt without the confidence I gained from Coach Marcy and her staff.

As you can hopefully tell from my narrative, I have endless "moments" from my years at GenuWIN, and so once I began to write, I had no problem filling 5 pages. It was essential that I be very careful with my word-choice because I wanted to honor my memories of Coach Marcy and paint her honestly, but still unique to my perspective. One of the best pieces of writing advice I ever got was from Dr. Russell on this assignment: use more dialogue! People enjoy reading dialogue more than narration, it's more relatable, and often it tells us more about a character than a descriptive paragraph ever will. I think that was the best tool I used in my explanation of who Coach Marcy is. Perhaps the hardest part about this task was deciding how to end and answer the burning question, "So what?" To first-year writers who have the same problem, I would say be honest, acknowledge the other side of the argument, and try to leave with something emotional and relevant to your audience. Beyond that, try to keep your sentence structures fresh and don't be afraid to visit your professor's office hours for a closer review of your work!

Hard Work Beats Talent When Talent Doesn't Work Hard

"C'mon old lady! If I can get all the way down, so can you!"

Sweat is dripping down my nose, my headband is sliding down my head, and my legs are burning.

Like drill sergeants, the other coaches call us out by name and drive us forward. There's no better way to break in girls at a catching clinic than the catcher crawl, the hellish warm-up that has us groping towards the other end of the field in a low squat. "Are you guys tired already? I think some of you are a little OOS!" Coach Marcy taunts us once we've all made it and waits to let the acronym sink in. It's only been 10 minutes into the catcher camp, and many of us are already questioning what we had for dinner. The other coaches give Coach

Marcy a knowing nod and she adds, for those who are new, "Out Of Shape!" Laughter echoes throughout the facility in between puffs of hot breath, and then they have us go back to the other side in the catcher crawl again.

I started attending Marcy's clinics just two years after my first hitting lessons with her. I was 10 or 11 years old when my dad and I first drove out to Marcy's place, GenuWIN Sports Training, in Romeoville. At that time, before we knew all the back roads, it took us an hour. We would pull up to the parking lot as the sun was just starting to fall, and I would carry my bag, always too big for my body, and walk inside. I can't remember whose maxim it was, whether it was my dad's or Marcy's, but I always knew that *I was responsible for carrying my bag;* no one else could pack it or carry it for me.

My dad liked to be early to my hitting lessons, so we would find an empty cage and hit balls for ten minutes. That way, I wasn't coming to Marcy to warm up my swing; it was all ready for her to mold. She would sit on a bucket, toss me a set of balls, and examine my swing with laser vision. Her stare was piercing, but her words were kind. Marcy is Greek and she grew up on the south side of Chicago, so she had a very direct teaching style. Almost everything she taught had a good story behind it. She would always start by saying, "Now listen Tom," even though my dad goes exclusively by Thomas, "If Katie were my daughter, I would have her do *this*." And then she'd proceed to share her pearls of wisdom with us, whether it be a brand of bat to buy or an exercise to do at home.

And there were plenty of exercises for me to do. To name a few: we got a punching bag so I could practice hitting hard at contact. We put up a net in our garage and I would do up to 100 swings a day in the summer off a tee. We wrapped black tape around a green softball so I could practice snapping the ball straight off my fingertips. I would do nightly push-ups to build up arm strength and daily jumping jacks to increase my speed. Of course, I never did any of these all together. But over the years I certainly accumulated my fair share of classic Marcy exercises. Her homework always had a scientific element to it because she truly studied the game, and so everything she had us do was mechanical, with the goal of building muscle memory.

Mechanics was a buzzword in GenuWIN. The coaches would always say, "You need to work on your mechanics," and if you weren't making good contact, chances are your mechanics were "off." I could still name a million drills and anatomize a perfect swing today, without a moment's hesitation. Knees bent, elbows pointed out in a triangle shape, bat held at a forty-five degree angle. Don't tilt your head or you'll see the ball at an odd angle. Watch the ball! Your elbow always moves first, not your wrist—elbow the midget! Bring that hip around! For God's sake, EXTENSION! Extend those arms, that's where you get your power. Extension, Katie, come on, babe. Follow through. Don't watch the ball. *Run.*

Coach Marcy was a scientist, an innovator, and a student all in one. She was always researching new techniques and exercises to improve her players' games. Even though most of her students were in high school or younger, she utilized Olympic training exercises and took advice from D1 college football teams. Above all, Marcy was interested in the spirit of the game and what drove us to push on. She would throw out motivational phrases like she was flipping quarters at her students, and I caught them every time. "The harder you work, the harder it is to surrender." "It's not the hours you put in, but what you put into those hours. Quality over quantity." "The game doesn't know age, Katie." She would say. "Right now, there are girls who are younger than you and girls who are older than you that are practicing harder and longer than you." "There are three kinds of people in this world: those who watch stuff happen, those who make stuff happen, and those who wonder what the hell happened." Marcy was funny, but moreover, she was incredibly wise about the game and wise about life.

She had always instilled in GenuWIN an enormous sense of positivity. In the winter, she would run her famous high school camps, the Mecca for girls of all shapes and sizes to come on Sunday nights for three hours to prepare for school tryouts. There were girls there that had already signed to Division 1 schools their freshmen year, and there were girls that had never bunted before. "I always respect the girls who come back to my camps." She told us after one of the clinics. "You don't know it all. There's always something you can learn. Stay humble." Just like in her catching clinics, we would warm up with dynamic stretches and start the hour off with challenging exercises. Once you made it across the field, the older girls would cheer on their line, give out high fives, and call out "Nice job, ladies!" "Keep it up!" "Stay strong!" Marcy wouldn't have it any other way. There came a point in the clinics when every girl was shouting and encouraging every other girl in the room. The indoor field was a riot; everywhere you turned, you were being spurred on by strangers who had complete confidence in your success. In this way, there was no hole for failure, there was no place to hide. Your body stepped up to the task, and you performed. I've never felt so sure of my body's abilities as when those girls at the clinic were cheering me on.

There came a moment in her camps when Coach Marcy would grab her bat and everyone took an infield position. And this is when the skin would break. She'd call out your name, you'd lower into a defensive crouch, and then it was show time. There on Marcy's stage, all eyes were on you as she took a softball and shot it at you with an inimitable force. *Bam!* Blink, and you've been hit with a grapefruit-sized bullet tearing towards you at 60 miles per hour. She was an expert with fielding drills: she'd work your backhand, your weak hand, place the ball just a finger's distance from your farthest stretch. She'd hit and you'd react. It was a simple process of survival, but it required every ounce of concentration and effort you had in you. Her favorite students dove for every ball. And once you had it in your glove, that wasn't the end of it. Get up, *quickly,* and make a good, hard throw. "We're going at game speed ladies. A left-handed slapper can make it down to first base in less than 3 seconds. You don't have time for errors." Everything about this drill was *time time time*. Every millisecond was crucial. I would mentally direct my energy towards the ball, and put all my being into a forward motion. This is where I learned how to trust my body.

When it was my turn, the room seemed to hold its breath and the air was silent. Of course, that's probably how everyone felt when it was their turn, but for me, the exercise was a spectacle. I was no rookie at a Marcy camp; she would twiddle her bat and literally laugh at the satisfaction she was about to get from beating the crap out of me. "I'm going to get you," she'd say snidely. "Bring it on," I'd say with narrowed eyes, and the battle would begin. BAM! A ball shot past my right hand. I dove for it, but it was just outside my grasp. "Again!" I'd force myself up, knees sore, body aching, ready for another rep. Marcy hated when girls messed up and then went to the back of the line. "You stay there until you get it right." She told us. "You are strong, independent women, so stop being big weenies." BAM! The ball hit hard to my left side now, but my glove beat it there. The round shape in my glove, an affirmation of my success, was all I needed to bring myself to my feet again, and with complicated yet effortless footwork, align myself for the throw to third base. The girls in my line cheered, and we would repeat the cycle.

Years later, my glove sits tightly wrapped in the basement. The bats and the net and the punching bag collect dust now, but sometimes they still beckon me to practice. For weeks at a time softball had been a part of my daily regimen; softball was all I did on the weekends in the fall, in the mornings in the summer, on Sunday nights in the winter. I must have spent hundreds of hours at GenuWIN, and I must have heard Marcy say, "Do it right or I'll squeeze your head!" about a thousand times. It might seem that it's all a waste now that I no longer play softball. What did I put all that time and effort into if softball was only a finite dream?

As I go on living my normal life, I can say that those hours were everything. When it's midnight and I still need to study, I remember Coach Marcy. When I'm forty-five minutes into a hellish workout and want to give up, I remember Coach Marcy. Coach Marcy, who taught me how to shake someone's hand and look someone in the eye when I am meeting a teacher, or an employer, or the head of the OT department at Xavier, hoping to be in their program. "When you feel like giving up, give more." I couldn't ignore her voice in my head if I tried.

Questions to Consider

1. Katie begins her narrative with a piece of dialog without letting readers know the identity of the speaker. What effects might this have upon readers? How did you react to this opening line? What response did you have to this dialog along with the description of her physical sensations immediately after?
2. In her reflection, Katie mentions that she was encouraged to use more dialog in this piece overall. What does using dialog do to aid her story? Would this narrative have been as interesting if she had told the story without quoting dialog within it? Why or why not?
3. When reading this story, did you find yourself relating to the experiences described? Or thinking about someone, or some event, that had a similar effect upon you? Why do you think people tend to enjoy hearing and telling stories? What is the role of storytelling in our society?

A Night in Africa

Jessica Stoll
Narrative Argument

Reflection

To come up with an idea for this paper, I thought about instances in which I related to the prompt given, which was to write about a time in which my freedom of speech was limited. I had several ideas, but eventually ended up picking this story since the trips I have taken to Kenya have been such a big part of my life. This was very beneficial to me, because it was easy to talk about a subject that is so close to me. In addition to this, it kept my interest, which helps because oftentimes the drafting process can be long. Speaking of, the drafting process was something I found to be most difficult but also most helpful. The process included brainstorming, a "zero draft," which is essentially an introduction and an outline, a rough draft, and a final draft. At each step, I got feedback from two students as well as my professor. I took these comments and altered my paper at each step according to what these people thought, and this significantly helped me to come up with a paper that was written in an interesting, concise manner that was also grammatically correct.

The biggest change I made to this paper during the editing process was cutting out large amounts of information that were not essential to the understanding of the story. It was hard for me to see what parts of the story needed to be included and which didn't, since I was there experiencing the moment. With the help of my peers and teacher, I was able to see what was needed. It was important that I did include every detail at first so that I didn't have too little information for my editors, so I would recommend doing this. Another aspect I drastically changed was adding the section that quoted the actual words I said to the Maasai. I did this by finding a script I had written prior to the trip of what I had memorized to say to the Maasai in the case that I had the chance to share my testimony. After my professor had suggested I add this, I added it, and I thought it was beneficial because it helped keep it interesting and authentic. So, for this paper, my advice would be to choose a topic you are really interested in, take each step of the process seriously, and make revisions based on each comment from your professor and peers.

A Night in Africa

As I nervously stood surrounded by a few familiar faces and many unfamiliar faces, I went back and forth about whether I should share what I believe in my heart to be true. I had been asked if I wanted to speak, and I immediately thought that there was no way I could stand up in front of more than 100 people and speak. I convinced myself that I was too soft-spoken, too unprepared, and too inexperienced. But, somewhere in me, I spontaneously found the courage to do what I was so afraid of and speak to my beloved Maasai friends.

To get to this moment in time, I had traveled with a group from my church to work with a Maasai tribe in Kenya. The Maasai still live in primal conditions, living off of the land and making no use of modern technology. They are an unreached people group, so for us, this meant they have never had contact with religion. Our ultimate goal was to evangelize to them, even though this could be considered a risky task, especially in a country like Kenya. To evangelize to them, we had to gain their trust through learning and practicing their customs. As they became more accustomed to us, we were able to go into the school and teach, serve them meals, and provide a bible school for the kids. Eventually, they were even comfortable enough to let us into their homes.

The last night, they invited us into their bomas, which is a group of huts clumped together. This is a very high honor, as this was probably the first time non-Maasai had been inside. So, they escorted us a few miles down to their home. They guided us through rough terrain and helped us cross jagged fencing. Upon arriving, energetic kids stood everywhere, hanging all over us and beaming with smiles. The adults filled our hands with chai and chapatti to eat and drink. They began singing and dancing in Maasai and Swahili, diligently trying to teach us rigid Americans how to do their carefree dances. We sang, danced, talked, and ate their food for hours. Then, they handed the floor over to the 13 of us. This was the opportunity for us to evangelize. Eyes stared at us as they eagerly waited for us to begin speaking. Our leader came forward first, sharing his testimony. As others in the group began to speak, I was asked if I wanted to share. This was somewhat surprising to me, since I was very young in comparison to those in the group, I am not a pastor like many of them are, and I had no experience working with a translator. But, with some encouragement, I stood up in the crowd of Maasai and began to speak. I stood close to the translator, saying:

> "Hello Maasai friends. I have enjoyed my time with you; thank you for welcoming me so generously. I am Jessica, and I am 19 years old. I have been a Christian since I was 15. At 15, I was at a very low point after dealing with the deaths of several people close to me. In this, I found the love that God has to offer, and I was baptized in Him. I cling to the bible verse 'Be strong and courageous. Do not be afraid; do not be discouraged, for the Lord your God will be with you wherever you go.' I tell you this because in this verse I find hope and strength to get through the hard times, and if you accept Christ you can find this hope, too."

When I was done speaking, I returned to my group and felt an immense amount of relief and excitement. I was proud that I came up with the courage to speak, even if it was simplistic because of having to speak through the translator. This experience got even better the next morning. My new friend Rueben came up to me as I was telling everyone in my group goodbye. He pulled me aside and said he loved hearing me talk last night, as it was easier for him and his friends to relate to someone closer to their age. He promised that he would "keep God in his heart" wherever he ended up, and he would share this with people he knows and meets. This had me nearly in tears, as I realized the fear to speak I had overcame had a purpose. It had reached someone. It had been well-received. It was taken to heart. This 5-minute conversation made the grueling 39 hours of travel, sleeping in tents, eating strange food, and not showering worth it. This was reassuring to me, since many times in this world individuals face hostility when it comes to speaking about certain topics, especially religion.

In today's world, speaking out about religious beliefs and practices often comes with a price. It is not uncommon to hear about people being ridiculed, mocked, or even physically harmed for speaking about their religion, even if they were doing so in a peaceful way. For example, all in the past 15 months, a pregnant woman in Libya was sentenced to death for having a child with a Christian man, hundreds of Christian school girls were kidnapped in Nigeria and were forced to convert to Islam, and 147 students at Garissa University were killed for pronouncing they were Christian (Sherwood). This not only happens with Christianity but with every religion. Muslims are discriminated against throughout the United States, Jews are mocked in some areas of Europe, Buddhists are not accepted in certain parts of Asia, and the list continues. Furthermore, statistics back these notions. In 2012, 20% of countries worldwide experienced terrorism based on speaking about religion, 47% of countries had record of religious abuse towards religious minorities, 47% of countries reported political hostility regarding religion, and all but 13 countries worldwide reported violence regarding religion ("Religious Hostilities Reach Six-Year High"). This idea not only applies to religion, but to other personal views as well. The news is constantly filled with stories about people being bullied, mocked, or beaten for their views on sexuality, gun control, abortion, health care, war and so on. In light of hearing about events like these, this makes people very reluctant to speak about their viewpoints, especially if they are around strangers.

For me in Kenya, it was dangerous to be publicly proclaiming Christianity, especially in light of several anti-Christian attacks that had just happened prior to our departure. In addition to this, Kenya is the number 12 on the list of most hostile countries for religion. This is what caused me to be so timid and reluctant; but, I did it anyways, and surprisingly, it was received well based on Rueben's reaction. This demonstrates how sometimes speaking out can be received well even though this does not usually seem to be the case, especially when looking at what is happening in the world through the media. The importance of the Maasai being receptive to our views is important for a couple reasons. First, it encouraged us as missionaries to continue our evangelizing, which is a fundamental part of being a Christian. Second, it was a factor in many of the Maasai people in that area later becoming Christian. Though not everyone sees this as being a positive happening, to us, this is important because this means they accepted what we said to the extent that they spread Christianity to other villages.

Contrary to what is portrayed in modern day times, it is possible for people to speak out and have their message well received, based on my experience in Kenya. I did not receive negative backlash like some people do today.

This shows that people should speak out about their beliefs, whether they are beliefs about religion, politics, sexuality, or anything else. There is a chance it will be received badly, but there is also always the chance that it will be received well. After having a positive experience, the next time I am with my Maasai friends in Kenya, I will have the strength to speak without nervousness and uncertainty.

Works Cited

"Religious Hostilities Reach Six-Year High." *Pew Research Centers Religion Public Life Project RSS.* Pew Research Center, 14 Jan. 2014. Web. 03 Feb. 2016

Sherwood, Harriet. "Dying for Christianity." *The Guardian.* 27 July 2015. Web. 30 Jan. 2016.

Sledge, Matt. "Muslim Americans Widely Seen as Victims of Discrimination." *The Huffington Post.* 4 Feb. 2015. Web. 30 Jan. 2016.

Questions to Consider

1. Jessica's essay begins with a description of feeling ambivalent about speaking publicly about her experiences. How does Jessica introduce the idea of "speaking under risky circumstances" in this piece? Where and how does she weave this idea through her narrative? Is this theme effectively conveyed throughout the story?
2. Narrative arguments rely heavily upon story to make the main claims of an argument and offer a "representative anecdote" for a larger issue or problem. How would Jessica's argument have been different if she had skipped the story altogether and relied entirely upon the statistics she offers near the end of her essay? Do you think that her argument would have been as relatable without the human element of her vivid descriptions?
3. As mentioned, Jessica uses supportable facts within her narrative to help make her point. Do you think that her research helped back up the claims she was making about speech being risky in some circumstances? What is the difference between making an argument as a first person narrative versus arguing from a third person, fact-based stance? In what contexts might one approach work better than the other?

Category: Exploratory Essay

During your research process, you may be asked to write an exploratory essay as a way of discussing and thinking through all of the ideas you have about your topic, once you have conducted a significant portion of the research. This type of essay may go by other names, such as a Synthesis Essay or a Research Reflection, but the purpose is similar: to help you think through and solidify your ideas now that you have gained some expertise on a topic.

Exploratory essays may be less formal than some other forms of writing and can read like a combination of a literature review with a personal narrative. In an exploratory essay, you engage with the sources you have covered in your research—often in the form of an annotated bibliography or similar assignment—and write about your reactions to what you have learned. This type of essay can help you put together the multiple sources you have reviewed in your research and be an intermediary step toward a more formal research-based argument paper. Although an exploratory essay (or similar assignment) may seem like an extra step in the process, or additional writing for you to do, it can be an invaluable tool for organizing and synthesizing a large amount of research. This can actually make writing your research-based argument easier and clearer, so even if this is not assigned, doing some version of this on your own may aid your writing process in the long run.

When reading these essays, you also gain insight into the research and inquiry process of these student writers. Often, readers only see the "finished product" of research that may have taken many weeks or months to conduct. By examining these exploratory essays, you can observe what prompted these students to choose their topics, how they engaged with their sources, what they did when they realized they could not answer all of their questions, and where they looked for additional information. Research can be a rather solitary endeavor at times, so by sharing their research methods, thought processes, and insights, Nicholas and Samantha can provide first year students with an even deeper understanding of what research in college might entail.

The first example of an exploratory essay is from Nicholas Rittenhouse, who probes issues of morality and ethics in "Pacifism: Vice or Virtue?". He begins by grappling with large-scale issues such as violence and ideology, and then shifts to talking about his own personal history with the idea of pacifism. Through these introductory paragraphs, readers can see how this idea, which affects everyone on the planet, can also have very personal roots in an individual's life experience. He initiates exploration with historic inquiries into the foundations of pacifism, always questioning the positions he encounters more deeply. In his essay, readers can follow his search for answers, exploring pacifism in different contexts, and seeking out counter arguments. By the end of his essay, readers see the complexity of the issue, and the editorial team noted that Nicholas continues to seek accurate answers, rather than easy ones.

In her exploratory essay "Phobias," Samantha Dabney starts with her personal experience with a fear of spiders and shows how inquiry into one's own situation can lead to an extensive research process. The editorial team found Samantha's inquisitiveness striking, and by detailing her research journey, readers can witness how she continued to dig for more answers, as well as her reactions to surprise discoveries along the way. Readers can discern from her research narrative that Samantha had to return to the library many times to find other sources, and purposefully chose to explore different sorts of resources, such as articles and databases, in her search for answers about phobias. As she notes, she wanted to give readers more than the answers they could find in a Google search, and as evidenced by her exploratory essay, Samantha was able to do just that.

As you read these essays, think about the ways that you have conducted research yourself and imagine what you might learn from observing the ways others explore a topic. These essays will also give you an idea of what research at the college level might look like; you can note the variety of sources that Nicholas and Samantha utilize in their inquiries, as well as where they go to find information. In addition, you get a glimpse of what inquiry-based research is; rather than seeking backing for positions they already held, Nicholas and Samantha show how engaging with questions can drive the research process.

Pacifism: Vice or Virtue?

Nicholas Rittenhouse
Exploratory Essay

Reflection

During your time in a college English classroom you will be told that there is no "right" way to write just before being taught specific outlines to follow and emulate. I know little about you, dear reader, but I know that it is very rare that a human likes being told what to do and how to do it, especially when the orders are transmitted under some artificial guise of creativity. The best piece of advice I can give to a student taking a college course that admits little rhetorical freedom, is to choose a topic for each essay (if given the choice) that has interested you for a while. This topic may relate to your major, something you read or watched recently, or it may even be something of which you are completely ignorant. If you find a topic of interest and there is ample information available and research to be done, then I am sure you will effectively minimize the pain under which the assignment will be composed. In college, there is seldom a more daunting coupling than a boring paper assignment and a student tempted by an endless supply of technological distractions.

Once you have completed the first step, the rest is easy. Upon finding serviceable sources, it is very important that they are read accurately and thoroughly. This may require a slow pace, but, unsurprisingly, it will be of assistance when the information is utilized within your papers. Reading has never been an arduous task for me, so I often spent my Saturday mornings doing the research for an upcoming English paper, enjoying every bit of information I learned. Because most of my work began early, I never felt pressed for time. I would recommend you try to avoid procrastination in this way as well. I know of some who thrive under the added pressure of writing with little time, but I have always found it useful to leave a lot of time for revision. Try to get to a point in which you are able to be proud of your papers when they are finished. This is your writing. I need not tell you that it is an extension of yourself, encompassing your thoughts, interests, and memories. Treat it as you would your body: with respect and dignity.

Pacifism: Vice or Virtue?

Violent conflict has existed as long as men have fought over a common resource, namely, food and that which is necessary for shelter. As the years have progressed and technology has advanced, we have seen these same sorts of conflicts on a larger scale yield uglier outcomes. Now that the world is organized into an intricate system of inter-connected nation-states that have similar goals and aspirations we see political and economic partnerships that are based on altruistic exchanges. We have seen this delicate framework crumble at times, leaving many people struggling to find a position that minimizes casualties. The ideology that is generally accepted in times like these goes by the name of pacifism.

At times in my life I have found myself identifying as a pacifist before really exploring the implications of that position. I fondly recall having the specific question of war justification posed by my father and recognizing my inability to give a clear answer. More recently, I have had to sign up for the draft. The draft has a notorious history of dodged assignments and ludicrous excuses from individuals. Personally, I am not too keen on travelling to a foreign land to fight so I have often found myself meditating about ways in which I would be able to dodge the draft if it was reinstated.

It is important that when one is confronted with a difficult question, a solid answer can be offered up at all times. The research that I am going to conduct is long overdue, but it will leave me more knowledgeable and prepared to take a concrete stance on non-aggression policies at the micro and macro levels, leaving me capable of forming my own stance without relying on others to choose for me. I would not like to see anyone put in pain at my hands. However, I refuse to rule out the prospect of that being required to protect my family as well as myself. Failure to adhere to this would result in my not being a pacifist in the absolute sense. This leads me to the heart of the matter: Can the denunciation of violence be justified at all times or just when certain criteria are not met?

When one is confronted with a common position like pacifism, it is interesting to look back at the roots from which it has grown. The Christian Church, before being endorsed by Constantine, was a strong figure in the push for non-violence (*Timeline of Christianity*). This was a difficult position to take, especially when Christians were facing harsh persecution at the hands of the Romans. In fact, Christians experienced 129 years of persecution between 30 A.D. and 311 A.D., beginning under the rule of Nero and ending with the Treaty of Milan (Religion Facts). Even before this, people of Ancient Greece had an indirect subscription to the pacifist position through their support of Aristophanes' *Lysistrata,* a play that depicts an Athenian woman who encourages an anti-war sex strike. More recently, Norman Morrison, a Buddhist monk, and Roger La Porte immolated themselves to protest the war in Vietnam. As pacifists, I am sure they wanted to end their lives in such a way that educated the public on the true nature of war. They were not alone in the fight against the Vietnam War, as nearly half the United States population thought it was a mistake to send troops to Vietnam during wartime (Gallup).

Today, it is hard for me to hear about the numerous cases of "collateral damage," a term used to describe accidental killings, without feeling a slight unease in my stomach. Most people are familiar with the phrase "friendly fire," which is used to describe the killing of one's fellow troops. However, even if most people know what certain vague terms mean, does this imply justification for news outlets to use them at the expense of the ignorant? I often find that during wartime, my frustrations target popular news media for not telling the stories the way they actually happened, but instead backing into a sea of euphemisms and non-information. How is the public to know whether they should support a certain plan-of-action if they are ignorant of the particular details of the conflict thus far? Joe Biden, Vice President of the United States, recently discussed his willingness to support military action in Syria, claiming he is ready to "take out" the Islamic State in Iraq and Syria (Apps). What does this mean? Is the United States going to authorize the flight of more drones or take the steps necessary to put boots on the ground? It is displeasing for me to report that these questions are often left unanswered.

This leads me to the question of whether pacifism truly is a morally irrefutable position, even in times of war. I often hear of the uselessness of the invasion of Iraq from people with whom I am very close. However, after the atrocities of 9/11, there was wide support for an invasion of Iraq. In fact, seventy-two percent of Americans supported the Invasion of Iraq as of March 2003 according to a Gallup poll (Newport). Did this attack on innocents provide adequate justification for the invasion of Iraq? Nicholas Parkin, a visiting professor of philosophy at the University of Hong Kong who obtained a Ph.D. in political philosophy from the University of Melbourne, does not think so. In "Pacifism, Supreme Emergency and Moral Tragedy" Parkin makes it clear that when innocent people are dying, the forces interested in alleviating these atrocities must be sure that they will do more good than harm to avoid a "moral tragedy." This struck me as a depressing mode of thinking, as it is impossible for military leaders to predict the future outcomes of their actions. What is more horrifying: the evil we know or the evil we don't?

I continued to dig deeper into the idea of supreme emergencies, which, on the surface, seem to warrant immediate intervention and revolution wherever present. Parkin mentions the case of Nazi Germany and the British response by Winston Churchill claiming that what he faced in Europe was, in fact, a "supreme emergency" (637). But was Britain justified in denouncing the actions of the Third Reich? Parkin believes that Churchill did not have a right to place the lives of innocent German civilians in his crosshairs in order to ward off the threat, because such a move would be a strict violation of the German citizens' right to not be harmed. However, Churchill could not just sit by and wait for Germany to mold Europe into an Aryan superpower poised to make the entire world its playground. Such a situation Parkin deemed to be a "moral tragedy," a condition that is so morally complex that there is no answer that will yield a total absence of innocent deaths. The agent who promotes warfare, like in Churchill's case, must be excused because any plan of action is considered wrong by Parkin's account (638).

Unconvinced that this is a sensible way to give justification to wars, as everyone is considered wrong by Parkin's account, I wanted to look for an essay that confronted a pacifist's views head on. After a short amount of time I stumbled across Mark Vorobej's "Pacifism and Wartime Innocence." In this piece, Vorobej, a philosophy professor at McMaster University, offers a critique of pacifist Robert Holmes' views of warfare and its contents. Holmes, an Emeritus Professor of Philosophy at the University of Rochester, holds the view that because all wars imply the killing of innocents, there is no war that is morally justified. Who is considered innocent? Holmes believes that a person is morally off the hook in a warzone if they did not contribute to the initiation of armed conflict nor the overall conduct of the war (Holmes 11). Vorobej is quick to point out in "Pacifism and Wartime Innocence" that this position presupposes an account of moral wrongdoing and responsibility, and different traditions develop these ideas in different ways (172). Vorobej proposes what he calls the Restriction Thesis to challenge the precepts laid down by Holmes. The Restriction Thesis claims all intentional killing in at least some modern wars can be limited to the killing of combatants (Vorobej 173). If true, this would effectively counter Holmes' claim that all wars are unjustified because they presuppose the killing of innocents. This conclusion is puzzling, as there has not been a war that hasn't yielded some number of unintentional deaths. Especially in a modern climate where scientific progression has led to bigger weapons and larger death tolls, the proposition of having a war that only involves combatant deaths seems unlikely.

The Restriction Thesis as described by Vorobej raises an interesting question: Has the augmentation of weapons allowed for the ability to target only combatants? With the United States having the largest military budget in the world, projected at $598.5 billion for 2015, it seems plausible to expect that it would also have the most advanced technology ("Military Spending in the United States"). This may very well be true, as the United States has drones flying around several countries indiscriminately. As Spencer Ackerman, the national security editor for the Guardian, points out in his article "41 Men targeted but 1,147 people killed: US drone strikes-facts on the ground" there have been numerous cases in which the most advanced tactics yield disastrous results (Ackerman). Are drones the most useful way of preventing innocent deaths? It appears not. It seems that this a supported tactic because boots do not have to be deployed so American lives are never placed into the equation.

Upon further reflection, I have come to realize that pacifism does not exist in times of war alone, but also in times of peace through state-sponsored punishments of transgressors. Jan Narveson, a philosophy professor at the University of Waterloo, describes the necessary measures that must be taken to be considered a genuine pacifist in "Pacifism: A Philosophical Analysis." These include abhorring violence wherever it is found, even if that means not fighting back if someone is attacking you or your family. She then goes on to admit that if one holds this position, state-sponsored punishment of law breakers should not be accepted by pacifists. Would societal infrastructures crumble as a result of this mentality? My guess is that they undoubtedly would, as there would be no way to deter people from committing violent acts (Narveson 265).

Knowing that there was something very wrong with this position, I found an essay that critiques it by J. Angel Corlett entitled "Pacifism and Punishment." In this piece Corlett, a moral philosopher at San Diego State University, confirms my interpretation: Narveson simply does not know how to deter crime unless everyone subscribes to the strict pacifist position (953). Corlett supports proportionate punishment, the act of matching a punishment with the level of crime that was committed, but does not know how one would go about punishing a leader who enters a war and kills thousands of innocents as a result. It seems that this would call for capital punishment, but would this account for all of the wrongdoings orchestrated by such a person? Maybe. Corlett is a proponent for a position he calls *capital punishment suspensionism,* a position that rejects the use of capital punishment until all relevant details can be sorted out and the arbiters of such a practice know that who they are killing is in fact guilty of the charged offense. Narveson, I'm sure, would discount all details when denouncing all capital punishments under review (Corlett 954). Are we able to construe the idea of capital punishment as being the ability of a state to force an individual to fight on their behalf?

Regarding conscription, the obligatory military recruitment of young males in times of extreme war, Narveson does raise a good point in "Pacifism: A Philosophical Analysis." He points out the fact the if we feel as though we do not have a right to defend ourselves, there is no reason to expect others to defend us (Narveson 270). From my view, this makes my placement under the protection of the United States military unjustifiable because I would likely not protect them if given the opportunity. Does anyone have a right to accept protection from others if they believe they have the right not to defend themselves? It must be clear that if one believes they have the right to be nonviolent, others have the right to feel the same way. Therefore, if one is a pacifist, they should not expect aid from others in times of need.

Although there are many variations of pacifism, they all seem to have different applications in theory and practice. Sam Harris, a neuroscientist and author of several *New York Times* bestselling books, questions the position of absolute pacifism, the philosophy practiced and preached by Ghandi, as morally untouchable. Harris feels as though this philosophy is immoral, as it allows for violent acts against one's family to go unchallenged. He elaborates, claiming that a single psychopath, armed with only a knife, has the power to exterminate an entire city of absolute pacifists (318). This directly questions the plausibility of having such a philosophy dictate an entire community. Is mankind to the point at which we can live without locks on our door? I do not think so. Psychopathy, as described by Harris, has no cure and humans are doomed if there is no way of suppressing inherently violent individuals. How do we suppress such a threat? Reason and compromise will seldom suffice, especially if the person on the other end happens to be insane and, therefore, incapable of feeling empathetic toward others.

To the naked eye, pacifism seems to be a position with which it is hard to argue. I am happy to report that through this analysis I have come to know more of the implications that come with holding different positions based on variants of pacifism. In regard to the final solution as to whether pacifism is justified, the jury is still out. I noticed throughout my analysis that in terms of morality, the ability to utilize the lesser of two evils provides justification for force. However, I have not read a convincing argument that clearly lays out the difficulty inherent in this responsibility. It seems that if war is to occur, innocent lives will inevitably be lost as a result due to insufficient military training and technology. I hope to see this reality become opaque as the years move on through the advancement of technology but, until then, it is important that we all do their part to encourage nonviolent attitudes while at the same time knowing when one is oppressed and acting accordingly.

Works Cited

Ackerman, Spencer. "41 Men Targeted but 1,147 People Killed: US Drone Strikes—The Facts on the Ground." *The Guardian*. Guardian News and Media, 24 Nov. 2014. Web. 9 Feb. 2016.

Apps, Peter. "Biden: US Is Prepared to Seek Military Solution to 'take out' Isis." *The Independent*. Independent Digital News and Media, 23 Jan. 2016. Web. 10 Feb. 2016.

"Constantine the Great Rules." *Time Line of Early Christianity—The Lost Gospel of Judas—National Geographic*. N.p., n.d. Web. 16 Feb. 2016.

Corlett, J. Angelo. "Pacifism and Punishment." *Philosophia 41*.4 (2013): 945–958. *Humanities Full Text (H.W. Wilson)*. Web. 9 Feb. 2016.

Harris, Sam. *The End of Faith: Religion, Terror, and the Future of Reason*. New York: W.W. Norton, 2004. Print.

Holmes, Robert. "The Metaethics of Pacifism and Just War Theory." *Philosophical Forum* 46.1 (2015): 3–15. *Humanities Abstracts (H.W. Wilson)*. Web. 9 Feb. 2016.

"Iraq Versus Vietnam: A Comparison of Public Opinion." *Gallup.com*. N.p., 24 Aug. 2005. Web. 9 Feb. 2016.

"Military Spending in the United States." *National Priorities Project*. N.p., n.d. Web. 9 Feb. 2016.

Narveson, Jan. "Pacifism: A Philosophical Analysis." *Ethics* 1965: 259. *JSTOR Journals*. Web. 9 Feb. 2016.

Newport, Frank. "Seventy-Two Percent of Americans Support War Against Iraq." *Gallup.com*. N.p., 24 Mar. 2003. Web. 9 Feb. 2016.

Parkin, Nicholas. "Pacifism, Supreme Emergency, And Moral Tragedy." *Social Theory & Practice 40*.4 (2014): 631–648. *Academic Search Complete*. Web. 30 Jan. 2016.

"Persecution in the Early Church—ReligionFacts." *Persecution in the Early Church—ReligionFacts*. N.p., n.d. Web. 09 Feb. 2016.

Vorobej, Mark. "Pacifism and Wartime Innocence." *Social Theory and Practice: An International and Interdisciplinary Journal of Social Philosophy 20*.2 (1994): 171–191. *Philosopher's Index*. Web. 9 Feb. 2016.

"War and World Religions." *War and World Religions*. N.p., 14 Feb. 2011. Web. 9 Feb. 2016.

Questions to Consider

1. In this essay, readers are able to discern the complexities of an idea like pacifism without necessarily deriving any clear-cut answers about it as an ideology. After reading Nicholas's exploration of his research, what kinds of research-based arguments could you imagine him crafting? What claims might he make based upon the ideas he has encountered and produced himself? Can you think of a possible thesis statement for a research-based argument based upon this research?

2. What can you learn about an inquiry-based research process by reading this essay? What kinds of questions drove this research? When did Nicholas know if he had arrived at an "answer?" When is the research process "done?"

3. Looking at the Works Cited list, what kinds of sources did Nicholas explore? If this were your topic, are there areas of research that you might have sought? Can you think of other directions his research might have taken? How do you think that Nicholas's personal experience with this subject shaped his research?

Phobias

Samantha Dabney
Exploratory Essay

Reflection

I came up with this idea by thinking of topics that I would want to research and think of questions that I have always wondered. I would defiantly suggest not to wait until the last minute to start researching and writing this paper. In this paper I put in 12–18 hours of research, writing, and editing. Also, have your professor look at your draft and get some advice on it. If you wait until the last minute, you will guarantee that you will not get the best grade possible.

How I went about writing this essay is going and gathering as many books as I could. Not having enough research will make writing it that much harder. I picked out one main question and answered that in my paper. The question then led to other questions that came about during research. Make sure that you define and explain everything; write like you are writing to a person who has no experience in the topic.

Phobias

Just like the majority of little girls, I was scared of spiders. I hated them and wanted nothing to do with them. As I got older this fear seemed to get worse, and now whenever someone says the word spider I shiver and hope there's not one near me. It's gotten to the point where looking at a picture of a spider, in a book or online, will scare me. Even thinking about them makes me just want to lock myself in a room to be sure there are no spiders around me. People would tease me saying, "oh look there's a spider on your leg," and then use their fingers to walk up my leg like a spider would, I would always freak out even though I knew that there was no spider on me.

This got me thinking about why am I so scared of spiders. What makes me so scared? Why can't I even look at a picture of a spider and not freak out? So I Googled it, like every person would today, and it turns out that the fear that comes over me was something called a phobia. Now I've heard of phobias before, like the typical germ and height phobias, but I never thought that I would have one. My impression was that phobias are just a fear that is caused by a bad experience, but I've never had a bad experience with a spider. This really got me thinking more about what exactly is a phobia? Where did they come from and how does one develop a phobia?

I went to the library and started looking for books on phobias. I found the perfect book by Ronald M Doctor and Ada P. Kahn, for the start of my research. *The Encyclopedia of Phobias, Fears, and Anxieties* is the book, and in it they defined a phobia as an "irrational, intense fear of a person, object, situation, experience, thought, or stimulus event that is not shared by the consensual community" (Doctor and Kahn 389). This definition made sense to me, as whenever I think of people with phobias I usually assume that they avoid the phobia at all cost. But what do they mean by an irrational fear? My fear might be irrational to my friend but not to my parents. So what makes it as an irrational fear? That got me wondering if I could find what qualifies as an irrational fear in the history of phobias.

The word "phobia" comes "from the Greek word *phobos,* which means fear, panic, terror, and flight" (Doctor and Kahn 391). The earliest that it has been seen was written in flute music by Hippocrates, who lived from 460–377 B.C. Hippocrates was the first to write about fears and a phobic person. I found this very interesting because from the very beginning humans have always had fear of some sort. Phobias can also be connected to witchcraft and demonology, and has been seen in Shakespeare's *A Merchant of Venice*. It is very interesting to me how phobias impacted our literature and history.

The history of phobias is very interesting, but what is meant by an irrational fear? What does the word fear even mean? So I went back to the encyclopedia and found the definition of fear, which is "an emotion of uneasiness that arises as a normal response to perceived threat that may be real or imagined" (Doctor and Kahn 232). So fear to me is being anxious or worried about a situation that is rational to be anxious about, even if it's imagined. That being said, I would define an irrational fear as someone being anxious or worried about a situation about which most people would not be anxious.

But is the only difference between phobias and fear the "irrational" in the definition? I knew I wouldn't find this answer in the phobias encyclopedia, so I went back to the library to find some more books on fear and phobias. There I found many books, but Fraser Kent's book, *Nothing to Fear: Coping with Phobias,* gave a very good contrast between the two. He says that fears are natural, quickly mastered, variations of how we respond, and variation of the degree of fear. While phobias are not natural, can't be mastered quickly, and there is variation of phobias from a mild phobia to an incapacitating one (Kent 19). This was interesting how there is a very fine line between fear and phobias; I personally thought that there was a bigger difference between the two. But thinking about it now, it does make sense. Phobias are simply a type of fear. Now that I have an understanding of the history and definition of fears and phobias, this makes me to want to look deeper into phobias, where to they come from, and how one is diagnosed with this disorder.

I had checked out about every book on phobias from the library and started reading, trying to figure out where to go from here. I was reading just to find something interesting to me. Then while reading *Phobia: Psychological and Pharmacological Treatment,* I found something of interest. I read that there were different kinds or categories of phobias. I always thought that if you had a phobia, it was a phobia and nothing more. There are three different types of phobias: agoraphobia, specific phobias, and social phobias.

Agoraphobia "results in a housebound person who is completely dependent on others for even the smallest venture outside the home and who has to be accompanied everywhere" (Barlow and Mavissakalian 4). This surprised me, as I never thought that one's phobia would get so bad that they aren't able to do things that seem like nothing to everyone else. What makes a person that scared of something that they wouldn't even leave their own home? What could possibly make someone that scared?

Specific phobias is exactly what is sounds like; having a phobia of one or several things, be it an animal or heights or needles. These would all fall under a specific phobia (Barlow and Mavissakalian 5). This to me most like what I think everyone thinks of as a phobia; a fear of a single object. Before researching I thought that this was the only kind of phobia. However researching phobias really opened my eyes to see that this is a more complex disorder.

Lastly, social phobias "include fears and sometimes avoidance of specific social situations and social interactions, including eating in a restaurant or in public, public speaking, and parties" (Barlow and Mavissakalian 6). I have always had trouble speaking in classes and presentations, but I was always told that it was social anxiety and not a social phobia. This makes me wonder if social phobia is a type of social anxiety, or if there is a difference between the two? Unfortunately, I was not able to research this I had other things I wanted to get to, but it would be interesting to look into that at some point in the future. The three different phobias did make me wonder how phobias develop. Are they biological or is it something else?

I once again went back to the library, but this time I wanted to see what online books or articles I could find. As I was looking, I realized that there is no definite source of the cause of phobias. There was an article on the overview on how the theories came to be, however. David McDougal says that "phobias can be grouped under three general headings: those that stress unconscious emotional conflicts, those that are explained phobias based on the principles of learning, and those that consider biological factors" (McDougal). I always thought that phobias had something to do with a bad experience, but the possibility that it's biological really interests me. It never occurred to be that there could be a disconnect in the brain somewhere.

Continuing the search online I found an article on the possible biology of phobias by Lea Winerman. She starts out saying that to understand where phobias come from, we have to understand where fear comes from. She states that, "New York University psychologist Joseph LeDouz, PhD was to pinpoint pretty precisely where to look for fear in the brain" (Winerman). The part of the rat's brain that they pinpointed was the amygdala, which has "a double pathway leading to and from the amygdala" (Winerman). "One path leads from a frightening sensory stimulus in just a few thousands of a second" and the other is "slower pathways travels first to the higher cortex before reaching the amygdala" (Winerman).

But when tested with humans, they were expecting to find "abnormalities in the fast track through the amygdala," but instead they noticed a more active amygdala when they showed a picture of a certain phobia (Winerman). From this they now think "phobias and other anxiety disorders are caused by some type of dysfunction in the amygdala and related brain areas" (Winerman). This was interesting, to me. I wanted to know what dysfunction causes it, but it seems like they don't know. I never thought that there would be so much science in something that seems like a simple fear.

On the other side there are many different theories on how phobias develop mentally. The one that is most famous, and of which I knew a little about, was Sigmund Freud's case study that is known as "Little Hans." I searched the Internet for a reliable source of Freud's research on phobias. I found an overview in a professor's lecture notes, Jeffry Ricker, Ph.D. that explained the set up of Little Hans who was very scared of horses and refused of leave the house. After assessing Little Hans' fear of horses, Freud concluded that the development of Little Hans' "phobic fear was due to the interplay of conscious and unconscious thought and desires in conflict with one another" (Ricker).

This theory, compared to the biological theory, suggests that in order to create a phobia the person has to experience something traumatic. The two different theories both make sense, and I wonder which one has more supporters. I strongly believe that some phobias can come from a horrific experience, but I also believe that some people are just wired that way. They have a phobia not because of a horrible experience but because there is something in their head that makes them think this. Phobias and anxiety disorders have been linked together in every book or article that I've read. This got me wondering if there are any connections between anxieties disorders, like OCD or PTSD.

I already had every book on phobias from the library, so I just needed to find where this information was in these books. In a book called *Agoraphobia: Multiple Perspectives on Theory and Treatment*, I found a chapter written by Leon Salzman about what obsessive-compulsive disorder (OCD) and phobias have in common. First I needed to define what OCD was and if there were any similarities in the definition with phobias. So I thought the phobia encyclopedia would be my best bet to find a definition. They defined "obsessive" as "repeated, unwanted thoughts or compulsive behaviors, which are defined as rituals that themselves get out of control" (Doctor and Kahn 55). And they define "compulsive" as having "compulsions go through repeated, involuntary ritualistic behaviors that are believed to prevent or produce an unrelated future event" (Doctor and Kahn 55). So together, obsessive-compulsive would mean something along the lines of someone doing rituals repeatedly to prevent or produce a future that has a good chance of not coming true.

So how does this relate to phobias? Going back to Salzman's chapter, he says that "the phobia is clearly involved with the individual's problem of being in control, of being certain and secure" (Salzman 31). Since Salzman defined OCD as people wanting control, it would make sense that these two disorders have a similarity. Salzman goes on and says that there "are four clinical possibilities in the relationship of obsessional states to phobias" (Salzman 31). These four stages all have OCD along with different levels of phobias, from very mild to phobias that are more prominent than the OCD.

I never thought of OCD or phobias as an anxiety disorder, I always thought them as their own classification of disorders. And I never in my life thought that phobias and OCD had connection to one another. But now as I look at these similarities I can see a very strong connection between the two. Is there any major difference between the two? Can you have one without the other?

I didn't expect to learn much when I started this research, as I felt that I knew what a phobia was. I was surprised when I found out just how much I didn't know about phobias. As I kept researching, I just found more fascinating theories and facts. Probably one of the most interesting to me is that phobias might be caused by biological factors. These facts and theories brought up many new questions that I never thought about, and didn't even touch on other common topics, like how to treat phobias, as well as what phobias are common and why. I wanted to stay simple, learn about the true root of phobias, and treatment for common phobias. However, I felt like those topics can easily be Googled. I wanted to focus on something that most people didn't know and never thought about. I was very pleased on what I found and I think it did answer my question of what is a phobia.

Works Cited

Barlow, David and Matig Mavissakalian. *Phobia: Psychological and Pharmacological Treatment.* New York: The Guilford Press, 1981.

Doctor, Ronald M and Kahn, Ada P. *The Encyclopedia of Phobias, Fears, and Anxieties, Second Edition.* New York: Facts On File, Inc., 2000.

Kent, Fraser. *Nothing to Fear: Coping with Phobias.* Garden City: Doubleday and Company, Inc., 1977.

McDougal, David S. *Phobias. Salem Press Encyclopedia of Health.* 1 August 2014. 25 January 2016 <http://search.ebscohost.com/login.aspx?direct=true&db=ers&AN=93872153&site=eds-live&scope=site>.

Ricker, Jeffry. "Section 4–10: The Classical Conditioning of Phobias."*PSY 101—Introduction to Psychology by Jeffry Ricker, Ph.D.* 4 February 2015 <http://sccpsy101.com/home/chapter-4/section-10/>.

Salzman, Leon. "Obessions and Agoraphobia." Dianne, Chambless and Alan Goldstein. *Agoraphobia: Multiple Perspectives on Theory and Treatment.* New York: A Wiley-Interscience Publication, 1982. 19–42.

Winerman, Lea. "Figuring Out Phobia." *American Psychological Association.* 30 July 2005: 96.

Questions to Consider

1. What were Samantha's original questions going into this research? How did her questions change as she encountered information?
2. Samantha mentions that she began her research process by Googling her topic. Do you agree with her assertion that that is what everyone does today when seeking information? What might be the pros and cons of beginning a research process in this manner? If there were no Google, or no Internet, how would your research process be different?
3. What kinds of projects or papers can you imagine coming out of Samantha's research? What other questions might she pursue if she were to continue her inquiry within this topic? Where might her research lead?

Category: Common Assignment

The Common Assignment is an essay that is required in all ENGL 101 courses at Xavier. Although the topic for this assignment changes periodically, the general parameters are the same. Students in all sections of ENGL 101 read a common set of readings on the topic that offer different viewpoints, and then form their own arguments or positions based upon these readings, as well as additional outside research. The Common Assignment is typically composed (or at least revisited and revised) near the end of the semester so that students in ENGL 101 have the chance to build their writing, research, and argument skills by the time they craft and complete their Common Assignment essay.

This essay has multiple purposes. First, it gives all students in ENGL 101 a standard set of readings and an assignment that is required across all sections, which provides continuity in both knowledge and skills in order to complete. Second, it gives the Writing Program a shared assignment to assess the writing skills of students in ENGL 101 to make sure that we are meeting our promise to students and the university to successfully teach a set of learning outcomes for this course. Third, it allows students to test their own abilities in research, writing, and argumentation after practicing these skills all semester. By completing the Common Assignment, you participate in an experience shared by all ENGL 101 students and help the Writing Program improve the instruction it provides to you and to future students at Xavier.

In Emily Carmack's essay, "A Message to Candidates," she uses the assigned sources, along with other supplemental research, to craft an argument about what candidates need to do to engage young voters. The editorial team was impressed by the way Emily directs her essay toward a particular audience—potential political candidates—as a way to focus her claims and effectively make her point. Rather than simply report on what other sources had to say about this topic, Emily uses outside authors to help back her own positions and claims in a way that is compelling, well-organized, and easy to read.

If you are taking ENGL 101 this year, you will have to complete a Common Assignment by the end of the term. Although your conclusions may be different than Emily's, her essay gives an example of how one student approached this assignment with a particular audience and situation in mind.

A Message To Candidates

Emily Carmack
Common Assignment

Reflection

For this paper, I read through the prompts given to me and chose the topic that I was most interested in and wanted to learn more about. Reading through the prompt, I was curious why young people don't vote as much and, if possible, we could blame the candidates for lack of engagement. First, I read through the articles of Robert Klotz and Abby Johnson, and I took a lot of notes. Sometimes it helps me to print out the articles and use a highlighter to note the sentences that grab my attention and which sentences could be used for quotes. I used the EBSCOhost database, from the Xavier Library website, to find my next article. I narrowed down my search using key words like "millennials," "young voters," and "candidates." The next source I had was from the Pew Research Center because I wanted to get a recent statistic of the population of Millennials. After I gathered all my notes, I organized them into sections and, eventually, paragraphs. During my writing process, my essay was edited first by myself, then a few of my classmates, and finally my English professor. The critiques were all beneficial and crucial to creating my final draft. My advice to first-year students would be the more people who read and edit your essay, the better it will become, but you, as the author, always have the final say. Write clearly and authoritatively, making every word count. Remember your words hold great power.

A Message to Candidates

We are the generation of smart phones, medical technology and cures, the Internet, legalization of gay marriage, and the first African American President of the United States. We are multi-taskers, students, social-minded creatures, culturally and racially diverse, and individualistic. Nevertheless, we are considered indifferent and disconnected from the political world by candidates running for office. Millennials are the biggest population of people since Baby Boomers. According to Pew Research Center, the Millennial population (people aged 18–34) is estimated to be 75.3 million, while Baby Boomers' numbers were around 74.9 million. This generation is powerful in numbers and political involvement would undoubtedly affect our world. Although young voters are perceived as disengaged, candidates need to engage Millennials to increase voter participation while encouraging political activism.

Millennial voting participation may be declining because of inconvenience, no instant gratification, distrust of the government, lack of interest, or disengagement by candidates. In this day and age, we strive for convenience and immediate results. Voting is sometimes inconvenient for college students who live out of state, requiring them to obtain an absentee ballot. It is also a process that takes days or weeks to complete, so voters must wait patiently for the outcome. Many young people have a general distrust of the government, due to growing up during a politically problematic era. Abby Johnston states in her article "Political Peril: Why Millennials Don't Vote," "Two terms of Clinton marred by the high-profile affair, two divisive terms of George W. Bush and the war in Iraq and two underwhelming terms with the Obama administration have been all that most Millennial voters have ever known. The lack of engagement makes sense." This skepticism of the government is rational and occurs in older generations as well. In addition to distrust, most young voters believe that their vote does not count in the long run. Millennials understand that the voting issues affect them, but they are "discouraged by a political system they have watched fail for the last two decades" (Johnston). They are accustomed to believe that the government will do whatever the government chooses to do, regardless of the peoples' opinions. We can not necessarily blame them for believing this, because, in recent years, this belief has been proven true.

In addition, some argue that young voter participation is declining because of lack of interest; I believe that this is not always the case. Tobi Walker in "Make Them Pay Attention To Us: Young Voters And The 2004 Election" states "… online voter registration efforts such as Rock the Vote and Declare Yourself reported that more than two million young people around the country downloaded registration forms" (26). Walker also explains how young people have allocated public engagement into two worlds: civic and political (26). Millennials are active in their local communities through volunteering, fundraising, and being consumer activists (26). Many are involved in political clubs in schools, volunteer at food pantries, and organize canned food drives. Some students fundraise for charities, while others refuse to buy certain products because of unfair pay to workers or animal cruelty. In contrast, they are less likely to be engaged politically through individual monetary contribution, political party involvement, voting, and contacting public officials directly (26). The absence of young people in the political process results in a lack of invitation and engagement by campaigns, parties, and sponsorship groups (27). Some young people are apathetic towards politics, but many do indeed care. Millennials are stuck; they are not voting because of the lack of engagement by candidates, and the candidates are not engaging the new voters because they are not voting (Johnston). Candidates must realize that they would be more successful if they campaigned to this demographic group, acquired their votes, and engaged them as American citizens.

Political leaders and candidates are not expressing issues in a way that resonates with Millennials (Walker 27). Young voters are affected by and interested in the concerns facing the world today, but from a different perspective. They care about health care, but along the lines of access to health insurance, not health benefits for seniors (31). Education is a main focus, but specifically the affordability of colleges and universities. Millennials are concerned with the same issues as the older generations—such as the economy, wars over seas, education, health care, and unemployment—but in a different manner. They tend to focus on matters that significantly affect them. More than 75 percent of casualties in the Iraq war were under 30 years old, the unemployment rate of 18–42 year-olds is twice that of older adults, and student loan debt increased by 66 percent from 1997 to 2002 (28). These statistics prove that young adults are more touched by these issues than politicians appear to believe. Candidates need to view these topics through the Millennials' line of vision in order to connect with them (31).

Politicians must think like Millennials if they want their votes. They need to air political campaign ads when young voters watch television (such as during *Grey's Anatomy* or *The Bachelor*), visit college campuses, recruit young people interested in politics to be outreach coordinators, and continuously reach out to both registered and unregistered voters (Walker 31). Young adults must be included in their mobilization efforts. Phone calls, political party events, and campaigning door-to-door can be both effective for older and younger adults (32). Social media and pop culture are other important ways to reach young adults (Klotz 24). Robert Klotz explains "young adults come to understand political issues from 'many genres (especially entertainment media)' and personal discussion" (25). Millennials are less likely to be exposed to politics through traditional media, such as nightly network news and newspapers (29). Instead, online chats, polls, blogs, and meeting invitations are more effective ways to reach the younger generation (36).

Once a politician captivates the attention of a young voter, one challenge exists: keeping it. To gain Millennials' notice and loyalty, ongoing registrations and mobilization should be implemented (Walker 30). Candidates need to continue to encourage political activism even on years without elections (30). Political activity such as communicating with public officials, writing letters, signing petitions, lobbying, and demonstrating peacefully should be heartened by political figures wanting to engage the public (30). Technology can and should be used to track, mobilize, and motivate new voters. As much as 50 percent of Millennials today identify as independent, which is extremely desirable for candidates (Johnston). These new voters have swinging tendencies, and the more likely a candidate can win over a voter, the more likely the voter is to identify with that party affiliation (Johnston). Candidates need to reach out and involve young voters both during election and postelection years. Furthermore, they should inspire them to become more politically active in their communities and in the political world.

Millennials, the next upcoming generation of voters, need to be empowered and engaged by candidates to unleash their political power. The decline of voter participation among young adults is reason for concern and must be addressed and fixed. Candidates should invite young voters to partake in democracy, voice their opinions, and be both locally and politically involved. Political figures must look through the lens of Millennials and connect with them through issues that are relevant and important. They should use media that are popular for young voters and challenge them to do more. For a generation that represents nearly one-third of the population, these young adults are transitioning into older adults. Therefore, the votes of Millennials can and will alter the country—if politicians listen and respond.

Works Cited

Fry, Richard. "This Year, Millennials Will Overtake Baby Boomers." *Pew Research Center RSS*. Pewresearch.org, 16 Jan. 2015. Web. 25 Apr. 2016. <http://www.pewresearch.org/fact-tank/2015/01/16/this-year-millennials-will-overtake-baby-boomers/>

Johnston, Abby. "Political Peril: Why Millennials Don't Vote." *Vox Magazine*. Oct. 29, 2014. Web. <http://www.voxmagazine.com/2014/10/political-peril-why-millennials-dont-vote/>

Klotz, Robert J. "Different Experiences of Young Adults and Other Adults in Mediated Campaigns." *Mosh the Polls: Youth Voters, Popular Culture, and Democratic Engagement*. Eds. Tony Kelso and Brian Cogan. Lanham, MD: Lexington Books, 2008. 23–38. Print.

Walker, Tobi. "'Make Them Pay Attention To Us': Young Voters And The 2004 Election." *National Civic Review* 95.1 (2006): 26. *MasterFILE Premier*. Web. 21 Apr. 2016.

Questions to Consider

1. Emily frames her essay by directly addressing a particular audience. How does this focus shape the way she crafts her argument? What might have she done differently if she were trying to convince a different audience? For instance, what would have been different about Emily's essay if she had chosen to try to convince Millenials to vote?
2. If you were a political candidate, would you find this argument compelling? What could you do as a candidate to heed Emily's call to action? Would you want additional information in order to be convinced? Why or why not?
3. Emily mentions that she received feedback from many different people during her drafting process and that this feedback helped her improve her work. If you were offering peer review to Emily, what advice would you give to her about this paper? How would you help her make this argument even more effective?

Category: Reflective Essay

Reflective writing requires students to take a step back from their own writing, thinking, and typical ways of interacting with the world in order to reflect upon how they do what they do every day. By reflecting upon the writing process, students are required to articulate the choices they make, the experiences they have had, and how they have arrived where they are by the end of the semester or academic year. Contemplating in this way can encourage meta-cognitive awareness, which can allow you to more deeply understand the way you think, learn, and write.

You may be assigned various types of reflective writing in your ENGL 101 and 115 courses, as this type of writing can be adapted to suit many different purposes. Your instructor may ask you to write a reflective letter when you turn in your assignments so that your writing process is more transparent. Or, you may be asked to write a reflective essay at the end of the semester, looking back on the writing you have done and what you have learned. Reflective writing can take the form of more formal essays with writing prompts and page requirements, or it may be assigned as informal blog entries or discussion board posts as homework. Because reflective writing has the potential to help increase awareness of your writing and thinking process, you may want to keep a journal yourself that engages this type of writing, even if it is not required for your class. Meta-cognitive awareness of how and why you write the way that you do can support you in gaining skills, highlight your challenges, and increase the likelihood that you will be able to transfer a skill from one setting (such as ENGL 101 or 115) to another context.

In the first reflective essay, Christina Peterman offers advice to first year writers in "Take the Risk," where she examines her previous work, including the Rhetorical Analysis of hers that is featured earlier in this book. (See: "How Cassidy Argues Snowden's Heroism.") Christina uses her assignments from the semester as a way to examine her thinking, writing, and research process, noting how her position on her topic changed over time based upon the information she encountered. She quotes from her own work in this piece, which demonstrates to the reader how her ideas are reflected in the writing itself. Her essay culminates in advice to first year writing students, to take risks and put in the work to create high quality compositions.

Sela Brazier shares her experience with first year writers in her essay, "Note to a Future Freshman." Like Christina, Sela suggests that college writing is not always easy, but that sometimes the greatest rewards come via the biggest challenges. In her essay, readers can see her reflect upon her writing process, and she makes a strong case for engaging in process-based writing as a means of success in college. Because she has just completed her first year in college, Sela is perfectly situated to give advice to first year writers at Xavier as they, too, embark upon their first year as college students.

There are many kinds of reflective writing, and in fact, you have been reading reflections from students throughout this book at the beginning of each student essay selection. These last two pieces present direct, actionable advice to first year writers from students who have been there. Because these are reflective pieces themselves, there is no additional reflection presented by the student writers before the pieces begin. Additionally, "Questions for Consideration" after the essays will take both essays into account.

As you read these two pieces, think about what you might learn from those who have come before and how you can integrate their wisdom into your own process. Through sharing knowledge, we can all help one another on the "write path" as you begin your college career.

Take the Risk

Christina Peterman
Reflective Essay

My biggest struggle this semester was choosing a topic to focus on for the Rhetorical Analysis. This is because I knew that topic would be one I worked on for nearly the rest of the semester, so it needed to be one I was passionate about, one I could write a lot about, and one I truly enjoyed learning about. All of this made it quite difficult to narrow it down. When I finally chose Edward Snowden, I had one big reservation going in. This was because I already knew a lot about the topic and thus had already formed an opinion. I was afraid that this would preclude me from being able to keep an open mind and address both sides of the argument.

In the first paper I wrote on my topic, the Rhetorical Analysis, I believe the one-sidedness of my opinions was evident. The word choices I made when discussing the side I agreed with would clearly lead the reader to be able to see my opinion. I did attempt to account for this however, by clearly attributing the thoughts in most of my sentences to Cassidy, such as when I said "Cassidy spends the duration of the article arguing why Snowden's actions were justified, necessary, and even heroic." Because I knew so much about the topic going in, the research I did for the Rhetorical Analysis was not enough to change my mind.

As the semester progressed, however, the amount of research I had to do greatly increased. I had to do copious amounts of research in order to write my Annotated Bibliography, and my research had to focus on both sides of the issue. Even this, however, was not enough to change my mind. It did help though, that as in the Rhetorical Analysis, I was able to attribute most of the opinions to those that wrote them, but I still had some concerns regarding word choice. At the end of the paper, as I wrote my Synthesis Essay, which could not be attributed to another source, my opinions were made clear with my explicitly saying "in the end, I plan to come to the conclusion that Snowden's actions were justified and heroic."

As I compiled my Major Research Inquiry, however, my perspective began to shift. I organized the material and in doing so needed to consider all of the information I had collected. As I completed this process I realized that my thesis needed to shift, I had come to a new compromise. My thesis changed from Edward Snowden is a hero to "Snowden acted in a desperate manner, and the way in which his actions could have helped terrorists reveal a deep flaw within them, but his actions were necessary to the growth and development of this country as a beacon of justice that should be beyond reproach." Looking back at the way my perspective shifted throughout this entire process, I would advise anyone about to go through this process not to be afraid of choosing a topic they already have opinions on. As long as they are willing to put in the extra work necessary to keep an open mind, there should not be a problem.

My one other piece of advice stems out of the way I came to my compromise in my final paper. One of the reasons I was able to see the issue clearly enough to come to a new conclusion was because of the way I chose to organize my argument. In class, three types of argumentation styles were presented to us: the Classical style, Rogerian style, and Toulmin model. Each of these models brought a different strength to the table and yet none of them suited my topic perfectly. Therefore, I chose a model somewhat in between the Classical and Rogerian, and I believe this is what allowed me to keep an open mind. Because I did not strictly follow the Classical, as I would have done if I had been forced to pick one, I was able to come to some sort of compromise in the end like I did.

In short, my advice is not to be afraid to take risks. All throughout my writing process I was worried about how I did not stick to any specific style. This can be seen in my conclusions in the reflective letter I wrote on the Major Research Inquiry, in which I noted that, "If I had more time, I would continue work on organization and flow. Although I have spent the majority of my time working on it and went to the writing center to discuss it, I am still unsure about the effectiveness of how I wrote it, perhaps because I did not stick to a specific style." Even though I was so worried and spent so much time on organization, I do believe that it paid off in the end. Therefore, I would advise anyone in a similar situation not to be afraid to take risks with their writing, because in the end they can pay off.

Note to A Future Freshman

Sela Brazier
Reflective Essay

Following the closure of my first week of freshman college courses, I grasped a pivotal, fundamental understanding in regards to my student career at Xavier University. Specifically, I comprehended a significant tool for student success: my education is my own and it is my responsibility to fully embrace, treasure, and utilize it. For a future, incoming freshman, I hope a similar realization unfolds for him or her as well. The realization of one's education as solely within his or her control, carries immense power. Through the completion of English Composition, I exercised power and control in regards to my Xavier education. Precisely, through whole-hearted engagement, I observed positive outcomes. I fully grasped my education by identifying useful tools for writing success. Through sharing my straightforward guidance, I hope to help an incoming freshman achieve success in college writing-based courses; I hope to help an incoming freshman fully embrace the responsibility of a college education.

Undoubtedly, college writing-based courses present expectations for students far from effortless and straightforward. College courses are demanding and strenuous. Yet, through English Composition, I realized a basic rule for growth as a writer and as a student: do not always choose the easiest prompt. Pursuing the comfortable, uncomplicated essay topic is a trap for countless college students. In order to achieve authentic growth as a writer, one must challenge his or her personal thoughts through the expectations of a professor. Specifically, improvement as a writer originates within the pursuits of a student. The semester's various assignments and expectations challenged me to grow intellectually. Choosing the uncomfortable, challenging essay prompts exemplified my pursuit of whole-heartedly grasping my Xavier education.

Intentionally choosing the challenging essay prompts demands dedicated work ethic from a student. How might a student display a commitment to his or her work? Write a detailed, yet messy, first draft. Follow it with a cleaner second draft, then a third draft or even fourth draft. A student's writing always presents opportunities for improvement and advancement. With the busyness of college life, submitting an essay after only one draft is effortless. Yet, I challenge incoming freshmen to thoroughly edit their work, even pursuing the input of peers. Taking the extra time and effort to do so, reflects in one's overall success as a college student.

If students are expected to put forth the effort in choosing difficult prompts and drafting, how might success additionally tie into such endeavors? Deliberately choose to write about your passions. Write about what keeps your heart beating and your mind growing. Write about difficult subject matters. Write about a cause deserving advocacy. By pursuing a topic of passion, a student better exemplifies his or her personal voice. Additionally, writing about an engaging subject matter gives insight into one's personal story. Oftentimes students overlook mundane, ordinary essay prompts as yet another college assignment. I challenge incoming freshman to utilize every essay assignment as an opportunity for reflection upon of oneself: one's passions, pursuits, and personal story.

To the incoming freshman, realize and remember that your college education truly is a fortunate opportunity and demanding responsibility. Grasp the prospect of learning, whole-heartedly. Education possesses immense power in regards to personal aspirations and ambitions. Next time you are presented with a difficult, mundane essay topic, embrace it. Write multiple messy, unorganized drafts. Exemplify your authentic passions within every single college writing-based course.

Questions to Consider

1. After reading these two essays, what is the most memorable piece of advice that you take away from this experience? How might you incorporate that advice into your writing process during your first year at Xavier?
2. You have read these two essays by Christina and Sela, along with the reflective writing of every student who contributed to this book. Thinking back on all of those reflective pieces, name three things that you found the most useful. Next, think of the three things you found most surprising. What advice would you offer to yourself in order to be successful as a college level writer?
3. Christina and Sela both address you—future first year writers at Xavier—as their intended audience. When reading their essays, did you feel as though they were talking to you, or had your interests in mind when writing these essays? Why or why not?